PYRAMIDS

 a beginner's guide

RONALD L. BONEWITZ, PhD

Hodder & Stoughton

A MEMBER OF THE HODDER HEADLINE GROUP

To Guy and Meriel Ballard, with thanks

Orders: please contact Bookpoint Ltd, 78 Milton Park, Abingdon, Oxon OX14 4TD.
Telephone: (44) 01235 827720, Fax: (44) 01235 400454. Lines are open from
9.00–6.00, Monday to Saturday, with a 24 hour message answering service.
Email address: orders@bookpoint.co.uk

British Library Cataloguing in Publication Data
A catalogue record for this title is available from The British Library

ISBN 0 340 75383 8

First published 2000
Impression number 10 9 8 7 6 5 4 3 2 1
Year   2005 2004 2003 2002 2001 2000

Typeset by Transet Limited, Coventry, England.
Printed in Great Britain for Hodder & Stoughton Educational, a division of Hodder
Headline Plc, 338 Euston Road, London NW1 3BH by Cox and Wyman Limited,
Reading, Berks.

CONTENTS

Chapter 9   Inside the Pyramid   73

Chapter 10   Your own pyramid   78

References and further reading   88

Note to reader: all measurements have been given in metric. Some readers may find the following conversion formulae of use:

kilometres to miles: × 0.62
metres to feet: × 3.28
centimetres to inches: × 0.39

INTRODUCTION

Why another book on pyramids? Surely there are enough pyramid books to build a pyramid! Books on the mysteries of pyramids, books on the architecture of pyramids, books on the history of pyramids... the list goes on. Yet most books on the subject of pyramids have one thing in common: they approach pyramids from the particular viewpoint of the author, and are trying to make a specific point. These books usually bombard the reader with endless pages of detail and data. While this is appropriate for such books, it is unnecessary here, where specialist theories are summarized. From the theoretical standpoint at least, we may take their point as being made!

This book is intended as a general overview of the subject, taking into account the latest theories and discoveries. This includes new material on the Maya pyramids, which is just becoming available because Maya hieroglyphics are finally being decoded. The richly inscribed pyramids and their surrounding temple structures are now some of the most abundant sources of information about Maya beliefs and history.

Pyramids are a unique phenomenon in human history, and there are a number of possible explanations for their creation. Indeed, it is likely that there are several reasons why they were built, depending on the culture in which they were created. While pyramids are mostly thought of as an Egyptian creation, pyramids also appeared in North America, South and Central America, and related structures were constructed in Europe, Britain, and Mesopotamia. So while this book uses the Egyptian pyramids as a point of reference, the subject is explored in a much wider context.

Writing a book on pyramids is for me a unique personal opportunity. Growing up in the southwest of the USA, my interest in the Indian cultures from further south in Mexico and Central America was a natural extension of my own culture. Even in my teens I read extensively about the Aztecs, Incas, and, of course, the Mayas. I was thrilled to discover that my father had been sent some Aztec artefacts by one of his teachers, who excavated in Mexico in the 1920s.

I studied geology at university, with secondary training in archaeology. From time to time I was consulted on the geological aspects of archaeological digs in the American southwest. Later, as a professional pilot, I often flew into the Yucatan peninsula, and visited Maya sites. I gazed into the forbidding *cenote*, the sacred well of human sacrifice, at Chichen Itza, and watched the sunrise from the tops of pyramids. And I had the extreme good fortune to be befriended by living Maya on the then serene island of Cozumel, and was taken to unrecorded and unexcavated Maya ruins, including a previously unreported pyramid.

My later travels took me to Egypt, where I explored a number of pyramids, and was able to meditate, alone and uninterrupted, for half an hour in the King's Chamber of the Great Pyramid. When I was writing my books on crystals in the 1980s, pyramids and pyramid power were never far away. Some of that experience is reflected in the final chapter.

Pyramids have intrigued and astounded people for centuries. Even the Romans made special trips to Egypt just to see them 2000 years ago. The antiquity of the Egyptian pyramids is hard to imagine. Even if they were built as late as 2500 BC, as archaeologists suggest, they were ancient even in Cleopatra's time. Someone once remarked that Cleopatra lived closer to the building of the space shuttle than to the building of the pyramids!

While I cannot pass on to you here the huge wealth of information available about pyramids, I can hope to give you a taste of the magic and wonder they inspire. Enjoy.

Ronald L. Bonewitz, PhD
England, 1999

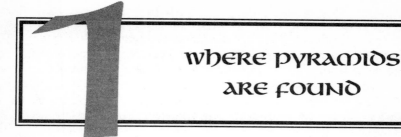

WHERE PYRAMIDS
ARE FOUND

On the windswept Giza plateau in Egypt, a tourist and his girlfriend stand before the Great Pyramid. She has been there before, but it is his first visit. He comes from the most advanced technical and engineering nation on the planet, yet he is in awe. Both speculate on how people in ancient times could have created such marvels. The tourist is Julius Caesar, his girlfriend is Cleopatra, and the year is 45 BC. Yet the pyramids are more ancient to them than Caesar and Cleopatra are to us.

On a sunbaked plateau looms another pyramid. Its base is virtually the same as the Great Pyramid's, but it is not quite as high, built to a different geometric ratio. Where the Great Pyramid was attended by priests in linen robes, this one was attended by priests in feather robes. It rests on a plateau a few kilometres north of Mexico City.

On yet another windswept plateau is a structure some believe to be a five-sided pyramid, and it is many times larger than the Great Pyramid. It is on Mars.

If we say the word 'pyramid', the associated word that immediately comes into people's minds is almost invariably 'Egypt'. Most people would be surprised to discover that there are pyramids in Mexico that are larger than many of the Egyptian pyramids, and there is even one that has nearly three times the bulk of the Great Pyramid. There is yet another pyramid in Mexico that may be several thousand years older than the oldest Egyptian pyramid. In this chapter we look not only at Egyptian pyramids, but discover all of the places worldwide where they are found.

3

Since the Great Pyramid, also known as the Pyramid of Khufu, is the standard by which all other pyramids are measured, we will begin there. (Note that the Giza pyramids are often referred to by the Greek names of the Pharaohs to whom they are attributed. This text prefers the proper Egyptian names; thus Cheops = Khufu, Mykerinos = Menkaure.) Along with five other pyramids, it sits on the rocky Giza plateau 16 kilometres west of Cairo, overlooking the Nile valley. It is, quite possibly, the most studied and speculated-about building in history. This is in some ways unfortunate, because it has given it undue prominence among the 'Great Pyramids' of the world. In Egypt alone, there are at least 46 other major known pyramids, ranging in size from relatively small to the Pyramid of Kephren, sitting just behind the Great Pyramid on the Giza plateau, which is very nearly its equal in size. There has been much speculation about the use and movement of some of the huge stone blocks in the Great Pyramid's construction, but all over Egypt there are literally hundreds of buildings containing massive stones. For example, the Valley Temple, only a few hundred metres from the Great Pyramid, contains single blocks of stone weighing over 200 tonnes each. And, sprinkled across the main temple-cities of ancient Egypt are obelisks, many of which weigh between 50 and 70 tonnes each. Thus, the routine use of heavy stones was far from limited to the Giza plateau, but was rather an everyday feature of Egyptian architecture and engineering. While the Great Pyramid is a useful marker and standard against which to measure other pyramids, to describe it as 'unique', as many writers do, is quite inaccurate. To be sure it has certain notable features, which will be examined in further chapters.

Egyptian pyramids tend to be arranged in groupings referred to as 'pyramid fields'. Most of the Egyptian pyramids lie in four major fields, all of which are within 80 kilometres of Cairo, extending along the Nile valley. The most famous of these is the Giza pyramid field, where the Sphinx is also located. There are two major pyramid fields south of Cairo clustered around the ancient city of Memphis. At Saqqara, 16 kilometres south of the Great Pyramid, is a group of pyramids which some believe to be more important than Giza. Here, what may be the oldest Egyptian-built pyramid is found, the step-pyramid of Zoser (or Djoser). It stands about 60 metres tall, and is

reckoned to date to approximately 2650 BC. It originally stood surrounded by an elegant enclosure wall, most of which has now fallen to ruin. In Chapter 2 we will examine the building of this pyramid, because within its structure lies a clue to the origin of the pyramids themselves. Nearby lies an even more important pyramid: the Pyramid of Unas. Although in a considerably ruined state, and several centuries younger than the Zoser Pyramid, the chambers of this pyramid contain what are generally reckoned to be the oldest religious writings in the world: The Pyramid Texts. These texts will become important in a later chapter.

Another 11 kilometres south of Memphis and Saqqara lies the Dahshur pyramid field, where the Bent Pyramid is located. There are a few lone pyramids sprinkled between these pyramid fields, and further smaller pyramid fields are found south of Cairo, but the most notable pyramids are in this area. There are other important pyramids in Egypt, several of which are noted herein. But for the moment, we will identify the many other places in the world where they have been discovered.

The major pyramid fields of Egypt and Nubia.

Mexico and Central America

About 55 kilometres northeast of Mexico City, one of the greatest mysteries of the ancient world is found – Teotihuacan. Here an ancient city is situated, at the centre of which is a cluster of three huge pyramids. Along a central axis, often called the Way of the Dead, the Pyramid of the Moon stands at one end and at the opposite end and slightly off-set from the centre of this avenue, the Pyramid of Quetzalcoatl. More or less central and off-set from the avenue looms the huge Pyramid of the Sun. In truth, no one knows what names these pyramids originally had, as no one knows who actually built them! None of the structures at Teotihuacan have been definitively dated: dates given by various studies range from AD 600 to as early as 1500 BC. Geological studies, however, point to an even older date: 4000 BC. What is known is that the Aztecs rediscovered and reoccupied the city in the twelfth century AD, at

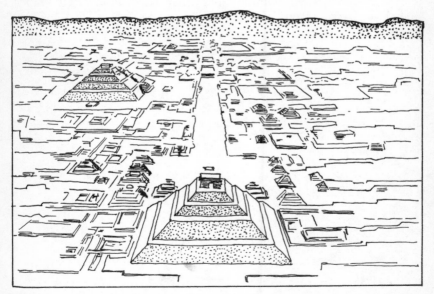

Teotihuacan, with the Pyramid of the Moon in the foreground, and the Pyramid of the Sun to the left.

which time it was densely overgrown, and scarcely recognizable as a city at all (Peter Tompkins, *Mysteries of the Mexican Pyramids*).

In Mexico's Hidalgo province lies the ancient centre from which all of Mesoamerican culture arose: the city of Tula, once thought to be mythical. Although still undergoing excavation, several pyramids have been discovered here, only one of which has been completely excavated. This pyramid, known thus far only as Pyramid B has on its temple platform, four granite pillars and four gruesome granite idols, each 2.7 metres tall. Around its base, to the north and east, are murals depicting jaguars and eagles feasting on human hearts.

Just south and east of Mexico City lies the sleepy town of Cholula, and its virtually unknown earthen pyramid. Now crowned by a Catholic church in place of its original temple, this pyramid, which once rose in four steps, is nearly a kilometre along each side of its base, and rises more than 65 metres. With a base area of 45 acres, it was three times bigger than the Great Pyramid of Egypt (*Fair Gods and Stone Faces*, Constance Irwin). At the time of the Spanish conquest in the early 1500s, Cholula was a great centre of pilgrimage, and had a population of nearly 100,000. The temple which once sat on top of the great pyramid was destroyed by the Spanish, and replaced with the church which still stands there to this day.

The story of the building of the pyramid at Cholula was preserved by a contentious Spaniard, Diego Duran. In 1585 he interviewed an elder of the town, who recounted the story of the building of the pyramid:

> *In the beginning, before the light of the sun had been created, this place was in obscurity and darkness; all was a plain, without hill or elevation, encircled in every part by water, without tree or created thing. Immediately after the light and the sun arose in the east… men possessed the land. Enamoured of the light and beauty of the sun they determined to build a tower so high that its summit should reach the sky.*

('Historia Antiqua de la Neuve España', Diego Duran).

The pyramid was not built all at one time, but rather in stages over perhaps a thousand years or so. Indeed, it may not have been constructed entirely by one culture, as the region was inhabited

variously by the Olmecs, Toltecs, Zapotecs, Mixtecs and Aztecs. Originally it started as a tall, conical pyramid with a flattened summit. A second layer was added over the outside of that, made of compacted stone, raising the temple platform to over 60 metres. Over succeeding generations, many more layers were added to the pyramid, but without increasing its height. Eventually it reached its four-layered step-pyramid shape. With its volume estimated at 3 million cubic metres, it is, quite possibly, the largest building ever erected on earth.

Some of the greatest questions in Mexican archaeology are the ages of not only the Cholula pyramid, but of the very earliest pyramids generally. At the very edge of Mexico City, lies another step-pyramid which was partially excavated in the 1920s. What is unique about this pyramid, is that it was partially buried under a lava flow. The geologist who studied the flow which buried three sides of the pyramid as well as 155 square kilometres of the area around it, concluded that the disaster took place at least 7000 years ago (*Mysteries of the Mexican Pyramids*, Peter Tompkins). An archaeologist from the National Geographical Society studied the site in the early 1930s, and stated categorically that this temple 'fell into ruins some 8500 years ago' ('Cuicilco and Archaic Culture of Mexico', Byron S. Cummings). To be certain, dating methods were not as precise during that period, either archaeologically or geologically, but it would be wrong to dismiss these roughly corresponding dates out of hand.

The Olmecs

So to whom do we attribute the oldest pyramids in Mesoamerica? The answer is far from clear cut, but strong candidates may be the Olmecs. Most archaeologists consider the Olmecs to be the 'mother culture' of Central America, from which the Toltecs, Maya, and finally the Aztecs ultimately evolved. The greatest mystery is where the Olmecs themselves came from: there is no evidence anywhere in Mexico of a developmental phase, nor has one been found anywhere else in the New World. Equally, we cannot be totally certain of exactly *who* the Olmecs were. Not one Olmec skeleton has been

discovered and even the name we give to them, Olmecs, has been assigned to them by archaeologists – we have no idea what they called themselves. As we will discover in Chapter 7, it is just possible that they may have been Egyptians.

The most impressive Olmec site is at La Venta, situated on an island in the Tonala River, south of Mexico City. In the heart of La Venta there were two pyramids, one of stone, and the other a fluted cone of packed earth, consisting of ten flutes. It was 30 metres tall and about 60 metres in diameter. These two pyramids occupied each end of the central axis of the ceremonial plaza, along which were aligned several smaller pyramids, platforms, and mounds, covering more than 8 square kilometres. There is considerable dispute in archaeology over the age of La Venta, but many believe it may date to as far back as 2000 BC.

The Maya

The Maya were, and still are, Central American Indians who form the greater populations of the southernmost Mexican states of Yucatan and Chiapas, as well as Guatemala, Honduras and Nicaragua. In the first centuries AD they began to erect some of the largest buildings in the New World, a highly sophisticated mathematics appeared, and they came into possession of a solar, lunar, and Venus calendar more accurate than any other calendar of the day. Tikal, in Guatemala, is one of the largest Maya cities and one of the largest ancient cities in the New World. It is also one of the earliest Maya cities, being well established by about AD 400. At its peak, the city of Tikal covered 15.5 square kilometres and comprised about 3,000 buildings, ranging from temples to huts. At the centre is the Great Plaza, with huge temple-pyramids to the east and to the west, the highest of which reaches 69 metres. Four other large pyramids loom over the rest of the central area. It is but one of many Maya cities where pyramids are found. No one knows how many as heavy jungle covers much of the area. It is anticipated that many other Maya cities are yet to be discovered, and the total number of major pyramids may run into scores.

North America

In the northwest corner of the American state of Georgia, lies the ancient Indian town of Etowah. Dominating the town site are the remains of three earthen pyramids, all of which were used as temple platforms in the same manner as the Maya pyramids. Like the Maya, the Etowans used these as both temple mounds and as burial mounds. Built as a pyramid with a rectangular base, the largest of these mounds stands as high as a six-storey building, and holds over a million individually carried basket-loads of earth. When excavated, it was discovered that it contained dozens of burials, some of which were accompanied by high-status grave goods, such as marble statues, pearls, and elaborately carved show ornaments.

The Etowan pyramids are far from unique. Similar mounds can be found at a number of sites scattered throughout Georgia and South Carolina, which were part of the same cultural area known as the South Appalachian Mississippian culture, which was thriving around AD 1200. The interpretation of these pyramidal mounds is based on the knowledge of the cultural beliefs of the peoples who inhabited the area: they served as 'earth islands', metaphors for the sacred landscape of mountains, caves, hills, and other world-symbols. The Creek Indians believed that the mounds invoked supernatural assistance and protection, their summit-temples serving as places for rites of purification. The Choctaw people of Mississippi have a legend of a great platform mound called Nanih Waiya, meaning 'slanting hill', which they regarded as the Great Mother of the tribe. They believe that at its centre the Great Spirit created the first Choctaw ('Etowah', George E. Stuart).

Java

As unlikely a location as Java sounds, it is the possessor of one of the most massive and highly ornamented pyramids in the world. Located at Borobadur, it was brought to Western attention in 1814

and partially excavated by Thomas Stanford Raffles (of Singapore fame) when he was governor of Java. Built in the ninth century, it is of solid construction with no inner chambers, and is estimated to contain 1.6 million blocks of stone. Its unique ornamentation is described in Chapter 3.

Nubia and Kush

Nubia, now Sudan, was the state along the Nile below Egypt, and for a relatively brief time it was a province of Egypt. Until the last few decades the extensive ruins found throughout Nubia were thought to be the remains of Egyptian trading outposts. However, Nubia was a powerful kingdom in its own right. In several locations, particularly in the area immediately south of Egypt called Kush, dozens of pyramids were built as tombs for Nubian kings. Slightly further south, around the ancient city of Meroe, yet more pyramid-tombs are found.

Mars

A pyramid on Mars? Maybe. Photographs from orbiting spacecraft have revealed an object that some interpret to be a five-sided pyramid. Nearby are other features named by some as the Citadel, a fortress-like feature, and a roughly rectangular hill that appears to be a humanoid face. The American space agency NASA, in response to speculation about these objects, released a later set of photos which appears to show them as natural features, with the humanoid face occurring solely as a result of the lighting in the previous photos. Who is right? Perhaps someone reading this will be the first to land on Mars to find out.

2 FORMS AND SHAPES OF PYRAMIDS

*W*hen *is a pyramid a pyramid? Pyramids are usually thought of as having a square base, and four triangular sides which meet at a point. Certainly this is the form exhibited by the well-known pyramids on the Giza plateau. Yet these are, in fact, relatively rare pyramid forms worldwide. Most of the pyramids around the world are of the 'stepped' variety. They usually consist of three to five 'layers' stacked one upon another, like the layers of a square wedding cake. In other pyramids the sides start upward at one angle, and midway up change to a different angle. Other pyramids are not 'pyramids' in the traditional forms at all. For example, the Olmec fluted cone described in Chapter 1, the Silbury Hill cone in England, and the huge pyramid at Cholula which began life as an inverted cone with a truncated point.*

Thus a 'pyramid' can be a wide variety of shapes and forms, but all are essentially an artificial mountain built to a given and pre-planned geometric form, and have been constructed through a communal effort in fulfilment of some religious or spiritual requirement of the society in which they were created. In the pages that follow, we will examine some of these forms more closely as we look at actual examples of pyramids that embody them.

Straight-sided pyramids are often referred to as 'true' pyramids. Among the pyramids of Egypt, they are the dominant form. Of the major Egyptian pyramids, 37 are true pyramids, nine are step-pyramids, and only one is a 'bent' pyramid. There is not a single true pyramid to be found in Mexico and Central America, where every pyramid is a step-pyramid. Many of the Mexican and Central American pyramids have general shapes and appearances similar to

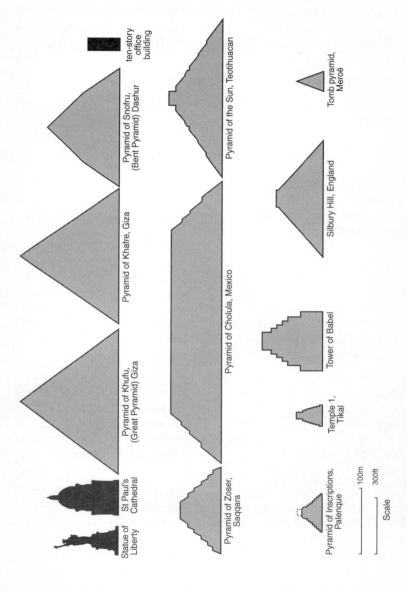

Statue of Liberty

St Paul's Cathedral

Pyramid of Khufu, (Great Pyramid) Giza

Pyramid of Khafre, Giza

Pyramid of Snofru, (Bent Pyramid) Dashur

ten-story office building

Pyramid of Zoser, Saqqara

Pyramid of Cholula, Mexico

Pyramid of the Sun, Teotihuacan

Pyramid of Inscriptions, Palenque

Temple 1, Tikal

Tower of Babel

Silbury Hill, England

Tomb pyramid, Meroë

100m

300ft

Scale

Relative sizes of pyramids across the world.

the Egyptian true pyramids, but others differ radically. In some pyramids, such as the Pyramid of the Sun, the sides of the pyramid form relatively straight lines similar to the true pyramid, but with very small steps.

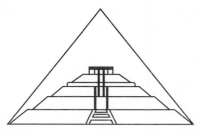

Comparison of the size and shape of the Pyramid of the Sun, Mexico, and the Great Pyramid, Egypt.

The Pyramid of Kukulcan at Chichen Itza, Mexico.

Others, such as the Pyramid of Kukulcan at Chichen Itza, show very pronounced steps. Others are built at a much steeper angle than the Egyptian pyramids. For example, the pyramids at Tikal rise very abruptly from the jungle floor at a 70-degree angle.

While most step-pyramids are a combination of steps with sloping sides, there is another form of step-pyramid where the walls are absolutely vertical in each step. Examples of these are the ziggurats

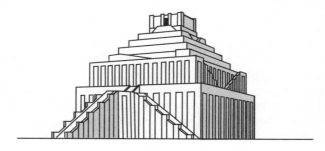

The tower of Babel.

The El Tigre group of pyramids at Mirador, Mexico.

15

of Mesopotamia. The tower of Babel is the best known, and appears to have been built to a set of very precise mathematical dimensions.

Neither Egyptian nor Mesoamerican pyramids were built in isolation: they were always part of either a pyramid group or a temple complex. In Mesoamerica this reached its culmination in the El Tigre group of pyramids at Mirador.

They are an example of Triadic Group pyramids – a large temple pyramid flanked by two smaller pyramids, all on the same platform. These groups are invariably oriented north–south, with the two smaller pyramids marking the equinox and solstice positions of the sunrise, as viewed from the larger pyramid. Such groups appeared at Tikal, Uaxactan, and several other cities in the core of the Maya lowlands during the Classic period, roughly 400–800 BC. Another type of pyramid complex which appeared in the Late Classic period at Tikal and a few nearby cities, was the twin-pyramid complex. On a square platform oriented to the cardinal directions, stood a pair of identical truncated pyramids along its eastern and western edges, each with a platform on top. The two pyramids represented the path of the sun, as well as suggesting the duality present everywhere in Maya belief.

In Egypt, the pyramid and its surrounding temple buildings are usually enclosed by a wall, often with smaller, subsidiary pyramids also enclosed within the same wall.

TRUE PYRAMIDS

As previously noted the true pyramid is a relatively rare pyramid form. The best remaining examples are those on the Giza plateau, although others were built in Egypt at Abusir, Saqqara, Dahshur, and Mazghuna. As we will discover in the following chapter, the construction of later true pyramids was much inferior to that of the Giza pyramids, and virtually all the later ones have fallen into ruin. The 52-degree Great Pyramid angle is repeated elsewhere in Egyptian true pyramids, for example, in the Pyramid of Snefru at

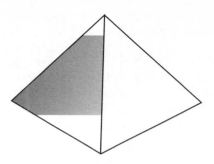

A true pyramid.

Maidum, and the Great Pyramid's companions at Giza, the Pyramids of Khephren and Menkaure. This is the only angle that yields a 2 *pi* base to height ratio.

True pyramids appear in significant numbers at one other location: Nubia. The characteristic that sets them apart from Egyptian pyramids is that they are very steep. Where most true pyramids in Egypt are built at around 52 degrees, the Nubian pyramids are closer to 70 degrees. They are stone-built, and many are well preserved. They are smaller than most Egyptian pyramids, the largest being somewhat smaller than Menkaure's Pyramid at Giza.

Step-pyramids

The step-pyramid of Zoser at Saqqara, Egypt.

The majority of pyramids worldwide are step-pyramids. Perhaps the classic Egyptian step-pyramid is that of Zoser at Saqqara. Not all pyramids are built on a square base. Many Maya pyramids are built with rectangular bases, like the Temple of the Inscriptions at Palenque (see Chapter 4). Other Maya pyramids are built on either square or rectangular bases but with extremely steep 70-degree sides, such as Temple 1 at Tikal.

Maya Temple 1 at Tikal, Guatemala, showing its platform, ascending stairway, and the remnants of the roof-comb top, an elaborate extension to add height to the temple.

Bent pyramids

In the pyramid field at Dahshur, south of Cairo, lies the only pyramid of its kind in the world – the famous Bent Pyramid. It is a large pyramid, and was intended to be even larger: the base of the

The Bent Pyramid at Dashur, south of Cairo, Egypt.

Bent Pyramid is exceeded only by that of the Great Pyramid. As the pyramid reached more than half of its intended height, the slope of its outer faces changed drastically from just over 54 degrees to 43 degrees, giving its blunted appearance. It appears that this pyramid was intended to be a true pyramid, but either construction flaws or problems which developed in a contemporary pyramid at Maidum caused its architects to re-think the structure. There is another unique pyramid at Dahshur, often referred to the Red or Pink Pyramid, so named because it is built of reddish limestone. It is one of the best-preserved true pyramids outside of Giza.

Conical pyramids

The largest of the known conical pyramids is Silbury Hill in the county of Wiltshire, England. It rises to a height of 37.5 metres,

covers 5 acres, and is built of over a million tonnes of hand-moved soil and rock. Archaeological investigations place the date of its construction well within the Pyramid Age, at around 2000 BC. The other major conical pyramid is the unusual fluted-cone pyramid that dominated the Olmec site at La Venta in central Mexico (see Chapter 1). Like Silbury Hill, it too was made from packed earth.

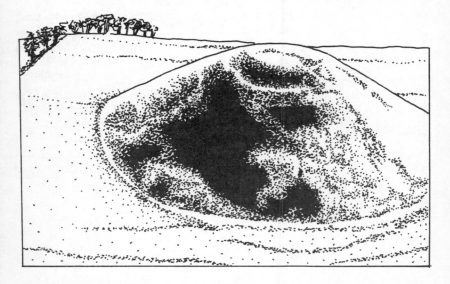

Aerial view of Silbury Hill, England, which dates back to around 2000 BC – well within the Pyramid Age.

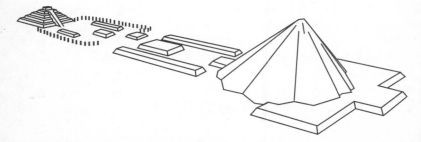

The fluted-cone pyramid of La Venta, central Mexico.

Changing shapes

Some pyramids change shape over time, and not just through deterioration and collapse. As we saw with the Cholula Pyramid, it began as one shape, and through numerous additions, eventually ended up being another shape entirely. This is not unique among Mesoamerican pyramids. Maya pyramids in particular often finished up looking entirely different from how they looked when work on them began. The Maya – indeed most early Mesoamerican cultures – used either two or three calendars running simultaneously. The two major Maya calendars were the 260-day sacred calendar called the Ritual Almanac, and the 365-day Vague Year. The start of the two calendars corresponds only every 52 years, a particularly sacred period of time to the Maya. The ceremonies associated with this time are called New Fire ceremonies, and as part of the rituals pyramids were refaced with new stone, houses were rebuilt, and there was a general refurbishment of the entire material culture. As a consequence of the refacing of pyramids, structural changes were also incorporated at that time.

Egyptian pyramids sometimes started as one shape and ended up another. The pyramid at Maidum was built originally as a seven-step pyramid, then altered to an eight-step, then its steps were altered, and finally a casing was built over the step-pyramid to turn it into a true pyramid. Other step-pyramids likewise appear to have been altered to become true pyramids. That they were originally intended as step-pyramids is shown by the finely finished outer faces of the steps.

3 BUILDING A PYRAMID

So, you own a couple of stone quarries, have a few thousand labourers available, and you want a pyramid. How do you go about building one? There are quite a few ways to go about it, but there are a few basic steps you need to take. The construction of some pyramids is a great mystery, while others can be easily explained. In the following pages we will look at the different ways of building a pyramid.

LOCATION

As obvious as it sounds, the first consideration of any pyramid builder has to be location. First, there is not much point in building it where no one will see it, so higher ground is often preferred. The reason for its construction is also a determining factor. If it is to be a temple platform, then it must be placed where people can get to it readily, for example, in the centre of a city. If it is a tomb it will be positioned according to local religious beliefs. A major factor must be whether the ground can support it. A structure weighing a million tonnes will displace anything below it that isn't very solid. The classic non-pyramid example is the Leaning Tower of Pisa, which is gradually sinking into the soft soil beneath. Enormous structures, such as the Great Pyramid and the Temple of the Sun, are built on solid rock, with platforms carefully flattened to give a solid foundation. In some of the more esoteric interpretations of the Great Pyramid much is made of its geographical placement. This may or may not be based on historic reality, but it is certainly true that

there was little option as to where to place it, along with the nearby Pyramid of Khephren, almost its equal in size. Anywhere else in the immediate area and there would have been nothing to build on but sand! Furthermore, the huge granite blocks in its interior, some of which weigh up to 70 tonnes, had to be transported to the site by water, so its proximity to the Nile must have likewise been a major factor. Wherever you put your pyramid, you must be able to get your building materials to the site.

ORIENTATION

Because the building of a pyramid was always undertaken as a result of the religious beliefs of its builders, some features of its construction invariably incorporated those beliefs. The simplest of these was in the orientation of the faces of the pyramid. The Great Pyramid, aside from any interpretative considerations, is noted for the precise orientation of its sides to the four cardinal points of the compass. Precise compass alignments are part of most ancient structures from a wide range of cultures. For example, Maya pyramids were always precisely oriented because of the belief that there were sacred attributes to each of the four directions. There was a similar belief in Egypt, where each of the four cardinal directions had its own god, collectively called the Tchatcha. They were instrumental in the passing of the soul from life into the realm of the gods, thus in any man-made structure dedicated to the afterlife important architectural counterparts can be found.

In Mesoamerica the entire layout of many cities was based on religious beliefs, as was architecture. There are very distinct astronomical alignments for the major temples and pyramids in virtually every Mesoamerican city. Buildings were believed to be gigantic living creatures, and were essentially artificial mountains, believed to have a life of their own. But individual buildings had their own alignments, often to a remarkable degree of sophistication. One of the most ornate and perfectly aligned pyramids in the Maya world is in the city of Palenque, and is referred to by its modern

name: the Temple of the Cross. It was built to celebrate the elevation of Chan Bahlum, successor to Lord Pacal, whose entombment exemplifies one of the functions of pyramids, as described in the following chapter. Its construction was designed to affirm that Chan Bahlum's succession was under the special auspices of the sun god. As the sun sets on the day of the winter solstice, its light passes through a notch in the ridge behind the Temple of the Inscriptions (see Chapter 4), containing the tomb of Lord Pacal. Its rays fall precisely on, and illuminate, the elaborate succession scenes in the Temple of the Cross. It is the only time of the year when they receive direct sunlight. As the sun sinks behind the ridge, it also appears to follow an oblique path along the line of the stairs, to Pacal's tomb. Thus the dying sun symbolically affirmed the succession.

CONSTRUCTION

The first stage of construction is the selection of building materials. Unless you have major transport – such as that provided by the Nile, you will be mostly limited to local materials. Many readers will have seen a picture of the Great Pyramid, built from row after row of fairly uniform limestone blocks stacked one upon another. While a number of pyramids were built in this fashion, there is as much variety in their construction as there is in their actual forms. Others were built of a core of rubble, faced with a layer of stone only on the outside. Yet others were built from beaten earth, or from mud-brick.

How solid, block-on-block pyramids, such as the Giza pyramids, were actually built has been a subject of ongoing controversy. This has particularly been the case with straight-sided, or true, pyramids. The problem has always been how the heavy stone blocks, some of which weighed many tonnes, were lifted to the required height. The only method known to have been used for certain by the ancient Egyptians was that of ramps. Ramps were inclined trackways built of mud-brick and rubble, along which the blocks were dragged on sledges, the wheel being unknown in Egypt at that time. But with straight-sided pyramids, if the ramp was built straight-on, by the end

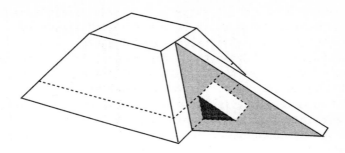

Straight-on ramp used in pyramid construction.

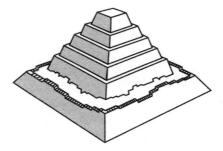

The step-pyramid core used in the construction of a true pyramid.

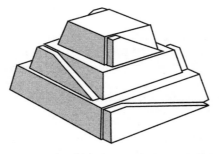

Parallel ramps used in conjunction with the step-pyramid core in the construction of a true pyramid.

of the building process the ramp would contain nearly as much material as the pyramid itself! More recently, it has been discovered that in most true pyramids, the straight outer sides are actually built over a core that is a step-pyramid. This much simplified the use of ramps, and provided a solid and stable internal structure for the pyramid. Assuming that the step-pyramid within was built first, the ramps would have gone from one step to another, alongside and parallel to the edges. The thin outer layer of the pyramid and its casing stones, much lighter than the actual construction blocks, would have been much easier to add on later.

But what about more esoteric methods? Some writers assert that the blocks were floated into place by mystical means, or through the use of crystals or sound. From an evidence standpoint, these theories seem unlikely. There are ample illustrations of blocks being moved on sledges or on rockers, but none whatever of them being moved by any mystical means. As dramatic as this must surely have been had it taken place, it is remarkable that none of the Egyptian illustrators picked up on it.

Equally mysterious from an engineering view point is the Valley Temple at the foot of the Great Pyramid. The core of this building is built entirely of gigantic limestone blocks, routinely exceeding 200 tonnes in weight each, of which there are hundreds. It is reported that there are presently only two land-based cranes in the world capable of lifting such weights. These are huge machines requiring counter weights of 160 tonnes and computer controls to maintain balance. For a single lift it can take up to 6 weeks of preparation time, requiring specialized teams of up to 20 men (*Fingerprints of the Gods*, Graham Hancock). In the Great Pyramid itself there are blocks of granite weighing up to 70 tonnes each, and located over 30 metres above the ground. Again, how were these moved?

In fact, the Egyptians have not been the only people to move heavy weights by hand. At the end of the last century Commander F. Barber, an American naval officer stationed in Egypt, who had an interest in Egyptology studied the problem of moving heavy stones. Because naval guns, weighing up to several tonnes, were still largely moved by hand at that time, we may be certain that the officer's study was based on practical experience. His conclusion was that 900 men

acting together could drag a 60-tonne stone up an incline. The size of the group would still be of a practical size, and would fit within the limitations of the known causeways along which stones were moved. Further, he noted that Egyptian illustrations of the time always show men – rather than draught animals – moving large objects. He concluded that this was a deliberate choice, because men could be drilled to work cooperatively together in a way that animals never could (*Secrets of the Great Pyramid*, Peter Tompkins). By pulling together in a surge, they could exert a force nearly equal to their combined weight, which would be, in itself, greater than the 60-tonne stone. Further, Egyptian drawings always show several men greasing the runners as the pull is applied, thereby lessening the necessary pulling force considerably.

There is evidence in the stones themselves of how the pyramid was built. Flinders Petrie (see Chapter 5) found horizontal lines carved on the casing stones and on some of the core masonry stones, showing just how the stones were to be fitted. His conclusion was that the casing stones and some of the core masonry were laid out on the ground and marked up by skilled masons working through the year and that, during the flood season when unskilled workers were available, the stones were raised into place. By laying out the stones of each masonry course on the ground beforehand, the precise fit of each stone with its neighbour could be assured before the laborious task of lifting them onto the pyramid. This activity would have taken many less men than the actual lifting, and it is possible that a small crew could have done this activity year-round. Indeed, many courses may have been laid out over the planting and harvesting season when the bulk of the labourers were engaged in agricultural activities. There is a further benefit to doing the ground layout: by the simple use of a long string running from corner to corner diagonally, the exact centre of the course can be accurately determined. By placing the centre stone of the next course exactly over the centre of the last already-erected course and building outward from the centre, an exact centre of the pyramid can be maintained as it is built upward.

The lifting and elevating of the heaviest monoliths *is* possible by a means seldom noted, but still used today. If one end of a monolith is lifted by use of a lever, and a block is placed beneath and just to

one side of its balance-point, the weight of several men downward at the elevated end is enough to tilt the opposite end upwards (1). While it is rocked upwards, a thicker block is inserted at the same position on the opposite side of the balance-point which is now slightly higher (2). Downward pressure is then put on the opposite end, with a higher block replacing the original block (3). The whole cycle is repeated as many times as necessary, with higher blocks being inserted at each stage. As the block rises, a pre-built platform is put under the centre as a higher base for the previous rocking cycles to be repeated. Those doing the rocking stand on platforms themselves, and the whole process in repeated until the monolith reaches the desired height.The writer has seen this process used on oak beams weighing over a tonne, but there is no reason for it not to work on heavier objects. A monolith weighing many tonnes can be thus elevated in a single day by a well-drilled crew.

Other Methods

As the Pyramid Age progressed in Egypt, yet another way of structuring pyramids was employed, which made the job easier and cheaper; the result, however, was an inferior product. Solid stone walls ran from the centre of the pyramid to the centres of each side, and diagonally to each corner. Other cross-walls created a series of interior chambers that were then filled in with stone blocks, rubble,

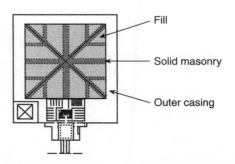

Plan view of later pyramid construction.

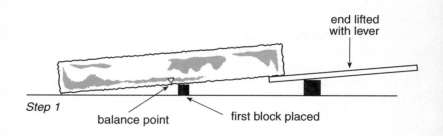

Step 1 — end lifted with lever · balance point · first block placed

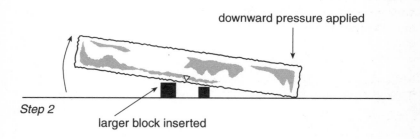

Step 2 — downward pressure applied · larger block inserted

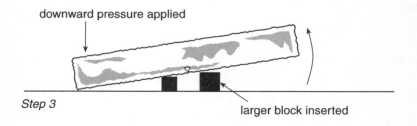

Step 3 — downward pressure applied · larger block inserted

Lifting a monolith using the balance-point rocking method.

29

or mud-bricks. Then, the entire structure was cased in hard limestone – like earlier pyramids. This method has proved far from durable, however, as virtually every pyramid built by this method has collapsed. Why was there a change in building methods? If the Giza pyramids were built at the time that Egyptologists suggest (the possibility that they weren't is discussed in Chapter 6), then they were built at the apex of the first flowering of the Pyramid Age. After the supposed time of their completion, there was a sharp decline in Egyptian civilization, leading to a complete collapse at the end of the Old Kingdom in around 2200 BC, the further implications of which are discussed in later chapters. At that time Egypt came under the rule of the Hyskos for a period. After the expulsion or assimilation of these unknown rulers, Egypt again returned to 'normal' – almost. The wealth and power of Egypt was a very long time in returning to Old Kingdom levels – long after the last pyramids were built. The inferior pyramids were almost all erected during this time of decline.

In Mesoamerica, both Mexican and Maya temple pyramids were usually built from limestone blocks over a core of rubble. As previously noted, in Maya pyramids at the end of every sacred 52-year cycle, a new layer of construction was added to the outside of existing temples and monuments, creating some difficulty in determining exactly at what point the Maya developed monumental architecture. Where collapse and erosion have exposed the internal portions of pyramids, one pyramid after another, rather like the layers of a Russian doll, have been discovered. The oldest buildings are buried deep in the centre, and often a rectangular temple building existed prior to the erection of a pyramid over it. These earliest temples were in many instance built several centuries before the birth of Christ at places like Tikal, Copan, and Palenque.

ORNAMENTATION

The ornamentation of pyramids is directly connected to their use. The Giza pyramids are utterly free of ornamentation. Not a single inscription has ever been found in them, and the few 'builders'

marks' found in the Great Pyramid are highly suspect. They were 'found' just at the end of a lengthy and expensive exploration of the pyramid in the nineteenth century, when not a single other discovery had been made to justify the costs. That the Giza pyramids were almost certainly never used as tombs is explored in the following chapter.

It is also true that later pyramids *were* used as tombs, but they are different in many ways from the Giza pyramids. They are invariably of poorer construction – so poor that in many instances they have collapsed altogether – and they are invariably highly ornamented. A classic example is the Pyramid of Sahure, in the pyramid complex at Abusir. The core masonry was of such a poor standard that the pyramid is now little more than a heap of rubble. But the higher quality stonework of its inner passages is better preserved and richly decorated. There are reliefs showing the king in worldly activities, his relationship to the gods, hunting scenes, and his return on a seagoing boat from an Asiatic expedition (*Atlas of Ancient Egypt*, Graham Speake). It is, in most respects, the equivalent within a pyramid of the rich decoration of the rock-cut tombs in the Valley of the Kings, an isolated burial place of later pharoahs situated in Luxor in upper Egypt.

The massive pyramid at Borobadur in Java is probably the most highly ornamented pyramid in the world. It is a step-pyramid, built of four square terraces surmounted by three round terraces. The walls of each terrace are covered with a total of 1460 relief panels, which together are more than 5 kilometres in length. The reliefs on these panels embrace the whole of Buddhist teaching, from the most basic lessons at the lowest level, to the most advanced teaching at the very highest levels of the pyramid. Interspersed with the relief panels are literally hundreds of Buddha figures. The circular terraces on top are crowned with a large central stupa, a stone structure in the form of a bell. The three surrounding round terraces contain a total of 72 smaller stupas, each enclosing a sitting Buddha figure within. Each of the seven terraces is a level of spiritual development, and only those at the very highest level would have seen the top terrace. The entire pyramid is, in a sense, a large school book for spiritual development.

This final example serves to point out what is perhaps the very first step in building a pyramid: deciding why you want one in the first place. While the building of the Egyptian pyramids started far back in antiquity, making it hard to be absolutely certain why they were built, more recent history elsewhere in the world may provide some insights. In Chapter 4 we will explore the idea of building a pyramid for 'spiritual merit', and how in the act of building a pyramid favour with the gods might be gained. Perhaps the pyramid is in itself a materialization of mankind's deepest spiritual beliefs. The Maya pyramids of Mesoamerica are a perfect case in point, as the next chapter reveals.

4

the uses of pyramids

It may seem strange to ask the question: 'What use is a pyramid?' Somehow pyramids are not usually thought of as utilitarian objects. Yet whole communities don't spend years constructing something that isn't, in some way, 'useful'. Indeed such an expenditure of time, resources, and effort suggests the highest of community purposes. But is it the same for each community and each pyramid? It turns out that the answer is 'no'.

Places of initiation

Many people have remembered past lives through hypnotic regression, and time after time the Great Pyramid has been remembered not as a place of burial, but as a place of initiation. It is true that other pyramids came to be burial places, but that was not the original intent. Within the Giza pyramids, there is not a shred of evidence to suggest they were used for contemporary burials: not so much as a single shard of pottery or scrap of burial offering has ever been found. If they were used as burial places, then the grave robbers swept up behind themselves as they left! The Giza pyramids are assumed to be burial pyramids only because of the stone boxes found in them, which are repeatedly referred to as sarcophagi in most references. In past-life memories, however, they are remembered as being filled with thick brine to support the body of the initiate in an essentially weightless state. (Modern flotation tanks use exactly the same method). Initiation is inevitably about

self-confrontation and self-testing. Isolation for a long period in the depths of a pyramid, with no sound, not a flicker of light, and suspended in brine to cancel out the effects of gravity, would leave the initiate with only him or herself for company. Add to that whatever effects the pyramid form itself might have, and the options would seem to be only two: emerge whole and centred, or be driven mad. That the latter occurred from time to time in poorly prepared initiates is also attested to in past-life memories. Indeed, such is the danger of modern isolation techniques, and psychologists who use them are highly trained. Despite this obvious use, that the sarcophagi may have been used as such does not seem to have occurred to orthodox archaeology.

In fact, the only Giza pyramid with even the remotest connection to a burial, is the Pyramid of Menkaure. There, a wooden sarcophagus was found which presumably contained the remains of Menkaure, but the evidence found with it showed that it was put into the pyramid 1800 years *after* his death (*Atlas of Ancient Egypt*, Graham Speake). The pyramid was refurbished around that later date, and presumably his sarcophagus was moved into it at that time. This brings up two important points. Firstly, his burial place was still well-enough known 1800 years after his death that his sarcophagus could be removed from it – most likely in a funery temple nearby, as accompanies most Egyptian pyramids. Secondly, if his burial place had been known for 1800 years, it was probably never meant to be in the pyramid, otherwise, even allowing for bureaucratic inefficiency, it would have taken somewhat less than 1800 years to get it there. Clearly, although Menkaure was indeed buried nearby, he was never intended to be inside the pyramid which was given his name thousands of years after his death. It is also evidence, at least in a negative sense, that the pyramid itself was never intended to be a tomb.

But as a place of initiation? Initiation has always been about testing one's 'right relationship' with the surrounding universe. In Egypt, this 'right relationship' was called Ma'at. In the form of the pyramid, each of the attributes of the four cardinal directions express the three fundamental aspects of Self – Love, Power, and Wisdom – represented as a triangle on the pyramid's sides. These are the three segments of *Ma'at* that must be in right relationship, and such

would have been the testing inside the pyramid. The pyramid then, is the four triangles of self-completion. When the three sides are equal (i.e. in the 'right relationship') it is the strongest form in the universe, and a person who manifests the three aspects in equal measure is Self-fulfilled. At each turn of the cycle of life is a new opportunity either to strengthen each of these aspects or to run the risk of developing imbalance – such is the challenge of growth (*The Timeless Wisdom of the Egyptians*, Ronald Bonewitz). Modern psychological theorists, such as Abraham Maslow, have noted that the attributes of a person who has fully developed their potential are much like those associated with deities. With certainty, a candidate-priest undergoing initiation would of necessity be tested for such attributes. It is significant to note that one way in which the Egyptians referred to pyramids was as 'The Place Where Gods Are Made'. The place of initiation of the priesthood was possibly pre-empted by the pharaoh, under the assumption that if it was good for the priests it was even better for him, although there is evidence that, at least early on, the pharaohs were themselves initiates.

Tombs

Because of the extreme age of the Egyptian pyramids, and the tendency for many of them to be reused at later dates, it is impossible to say for certain exactly how many of them were intended as tombs at the very beginning. A large number of Egyptian pyramids have, as part of their surrounding structures, a mortuary temple which was clearly intended to be a burial place. Some pyramids we can be certain of in this context, such as the pyramid of Sahure, mentioned in the last chapter.

The Step-Pyramid of Zoser at Saqqara is reckoned to have been built some time around 2600 BC. It is almost certainly the very first Egyptian-built pyramid, and perhaps the earliest stone structure of its size in the world. Evidence that it is the first of its kind is shown by the hesitation of its builders in developing its final form – six different plans are identifiable in the course of its construction. The 'invention' of the pyramid was credited by later Greek writers to the

legendary Imhotep, long thought to be a purely mythological character. However, during excavations at the pyramid in 1926, the name of Imhotep was actually found inscribed on the pedestal of a statue of Zoser, corroborating the ancient legend.

Near the southwest corner of the Step-Pyramid lies the smaller pyramid of Unas (or Wenis), wherein are found the most important Egyptian documents, and the oldest religious writings in the world, called the Pyramid Texts. In stark contrast to the utterly barren and uninscribed pyramids at Giza, the hieroglyph-lined chambers consist of two rectangular rooms covered by a gabled ceiling, painted with hundreds of stars. On the walls, row after row of hieroglyphic texts in an archaic form of Egyptian lay out the religious belief of the time, with references to even older material. Several other small pyramids nearby also contain additional versions of the texts, including the Pyramids of Pepi I, Pepi II, Neferikara, and Teti. This is their first known use within a pyramid, although they became a standard feature of most Egyptian pyramids built after this time. All of these pyramids containing the texts were clearly intended as tombs. The Pyramid Texts have proven to be the key to unravelling one of the mysteries of the Giza pyramids, as we will discover in Chapter 6.

Temple-platforms

In Mesoamerica pyramids as temples differed not only in shape, but also in use, from Egyptian pyramids. In the former, sacred activities took place on the outside rather than on the inside. In fact, the pyramid was used as a rather elaborate base upon which to set the temple itself. On the platforms on top of the pyramids, the temples contain one or more corbelled and plaster-covered rooms. They were small and cramped, and were used only on sacred occasions, when priests performed within them the rituals not meant for public eyes. Inscriptions indicate that they were also 'sleeping places', a term referring to divination. It was believed that dreams revealed the future, and that the condition of meditative or trance states was a sleep-like state in which the seer was 'sleeping'. For the Maya this included drug-induced visions.

To create a more impressive structure, the temples atop the pyramid platforms were heightened through the addition of a roof 'comb' – imposing and highly ornamented structures often taller than the temple building, and so named because of their resemblance to the tall, ornamental hair-combs worn by Spanish women in formal dress. Within the extensive carving and relief-work on these combs were illustrated stories relating to the gods, and to Mesoamerican mythology. Thus the temple became in itself an embodiment of Mesoamerican belief.

Both tombs and temple-platforms

Mesoamericans, and the Maya in particular, believed that the dead had a major influence over the living, and the burial of a powerful ruler within a major temple-pyramid was a way of keeping the old

Temple of the Inscriptions, Palenque, Mexico.

ruler close by to influence the new ruler. A classic example of this is in the Maya city of Palenque.

As we discovered in the last chapter, Lord Pacal, a ruler of the city who died in AD 683, is buried in a crypt in the Temple of the Inscriptions. The stairway down into the pyramid where his crypt is located was filled with rubble and sealed, but a slender pottery tube rose from the crypt to the temple rooms above, to allow for easier communication. Pacal has, in some respects, become a sort of Maya Tutankhamun. The large stone slab covering his sarcophagus is elaborately carved, showing a figure of Pacal amid a profusion of Maya symbols. This has been interpreted as everything up to and including it being a picture of an ancient astronaut!

Self-aggrandizement

In the tenth century AD, the Toltecs were driven out of the 'Rome of Mesoamerica', Tula, north of Mexico City, by the conquering Chichimecs. Moving further south, they in turn alighted on the Maya cities of northern Yucatan. A small, still-growing city, called Seven Bushes, was quickly overrun in AD 983. It was renamed Chichen. Later to be conquered by the Itzas, it is the now-famous city of Chichen Itza. The leader of the Toltecs modestly called himself Kukulcan, after an ancient Toltec god. Kukulcan quickly built a pyramid to honour himself, which is today still called the Pyramid of Kukulcan (see Chapter 2). His pyramid rises nearly 30 metres into the air, and has four stairways with 91 steps each. The top platform which also counts as a step, gives a total number of 365 steps, the number of days in the Maya and Toltec solar year. The design and orientation of the pyramid are such that at the spring and autumn equinoxes, patterns of light and shadow combine to create the illusion of a huge serpent rising up the northern staircase.

An unknown use

The only pyramid thus far reported from South America, the
Akatama Pyramid, lies in the ancient city of Tiahuanaco, in Bolivia.
It was oriented precisely toward the cardinal points, and measured
roughly 210 metres on each side. Originally it was a step-pyramid of
earth faced with large stone blocks. Since the Spanish conquest the
pyramid has been quarried for these blocks, and only a small
portion of them remain at the site. The pyramid is one among many
mysteries of the ancient city, for deep within it is a network of
zigzagging stone channels, meticulously angled and jointed, and
intended to serve as water channels from the large reservoir at the
top of the structure. The purpose of all of this is a great mystery, and
there has been much speculation about it by archaeologists, none of
which is definitive. Theories range from an unusual method of
human sacrifice to a system for washing ore (*Fingerprints of the
Gods*, Graham Hancock).

Spiritual merit

The construction of the massive pyramid at Borobadur in Java
brings to light an often ignored use of and reason for the building of
a pyramid: to gain spiritual merit for its builders. Although this
specific term is Buddhist, its general principle may well apply to the
builders of many of the pyramids worldwide: that in the
participation of the building of a holy place, those who work upon it
personally gain credit with whatever god or gods the building is
being constructed in homage to. Thus it is not simply a 'construction
job', but an act of faith, and in many instances, an actual act of
worship. We know from historical writings, that many of those who
built the great cathedrals of Europe had similar feelings of taking
part in a holy work. The Hollywood image of thousands of slaves
being driven by whip-wielding overseers as the pyramids climb
painfully into the sky may be purely that – Hollywood invention.
Indeed, many of the builders were quite willing, or even eager,

participants. Thus, whatever its final intended use, the actual construction of the pyramid was of benefit to the community on a day-to-day basis as it was being built. The possession by a community of such a building must have been considered to bring long-term benefits as well, thus bringing spiritual merit to the whole community, as well as to the actual builders.

Many uses

The building of pyramids for both spiritual merit and as an expression of religious belief, combined with its function as a means of communicating with the gods, is well illustrated in the Maya pyramids. The Maya word for pyramid is *kaqja*, literally meaning 'red house' (pyramids were usually painted red). For the Maya pyramids were, in effect, artificial mountains. Mountains were believed to hold up the sky itself, where the *Pauahtuns*, the gods on whom the weight of the world rests (the Maya equivalents of Atlas) resided. Not only that, the association of the colour red with pyramids reflects their often primary use: as places of human sacrifice. While this sounds grisly, a closer look at Maya belief gives us an insight in to the sort of religious purposes and the strength of belief that motivated pyramid builders all over the world.

The Maya perfectly understood the esoteric truism 'as above, so below' – meaning that all levels of reality from the smallest to the largest are reflections of each other. For example, reflecting their belief that the sky is held up at each of its four corners by a god, the house with its four corners may symbolize the universe itself. What happens within that house should, as a consequence, reflect the harmony and order of the universe. Similarly, a maize field with its four corners, or the community itself – held up by its 'pillars' – should likewise reflect the universal harmony and order. Equally, cosmic scales and distances can be reduced to earthly proportions in order that man can both comprehend and be at one with them: Maya cities are laid out on this basis, and so are the pyramids within them. This forms part of their deep understanding of the need

for balance and harmony in all things: imbalance and discord were believed to be at the root of all ills – individual, social, and even planetary. The whole of Maya civilization was geared to maintaining moderation and balance. All life was seen to be the gift and granting of the gods, and therefore it was necessary to give life in return, to balance the equation. Blood was believed to be life itself, and thus was an appropriate gift to the gods to balance the gift of life. An individual balanced his own life through ritual bloodletting, and the community balanced its life through ritual human sacrifice. Because something small could represent something large in the greater scheme of things, an individual's blood released through sacrifice could represent the blood of the whole community. In the comparative study of modern religious belief across its whole spectrum, the idea of sacrifice is embodied in all religions. The willingness to give up one's life, either ritually through service, or in some cases literally, is seen as the highest spiritual act. By offering the sacrifice at the top of the symbolic mountain – the pyramid, which was itself placed at the centre of the community and therefore in the symbolic centre of the universe – the sacrifice was literally delivered into the hands of the gods. This was a high honour, and the Maya sacrificial victims were not always unwilling by any means.

The Mother Mountain

Wherever they have been built, pyramids are, in almost every instance, an artificial mountain believed to have the attributes of whatever holy mountain or mountains are sacred to the local culture. The inner chambers of pyramids are artificial caves, with their own meaning. In the days of 'mother goddess' religions, entering the cave was 'entering' the earth, in order to become one with it. The practice of burying the dead is likely to originate in this symbolic return to earth's womb.

Mountains as dwelling places of divinities has been a common theme among most human cultures. The Indians of North and South America revered certain mountains, and the Incas in Peru even sacrificed small children to them: their bodies, mummified by the cold and dry air at the high altitudes of the sacred peaks, have been found. The Maya believed mountains to be living beings, along with their pyramids and other buildings. In ancient Greece, the gods lived on Mount Olympus, and Moses brought down the Ten Commandments from Mount Sinai.

Among other possibilities, the first pyramids in Egypt may have been erected as symbolic of the primordial hillock where the god Re stood when he created the first land from the swirling wasteland of water. It is even possible that if the Great Pyramid existed as early as 10,500 BC as some researchers suggest, then this may have been believed by later Egyptians to be *literally* the primordial hillock.

5

PYRAMIÐOLOGY
AND THE GREAT
PYRAMID

In this chapter we will begin to look at the more esoteric study of pyramids, both in the proper use of the term 'pyramidology', and its more general sense. Pyramidology emerged from a theory proposed by Englishman John Taylor in 1859. It was championed and further developed by no less than the Astronomer Royal, Charles Smith. In 1864 Smith proposed that the Great Pyramid was built to embody certain facets of an ancient, highly advanced knowledge. Before long others got involved, notably Piazzi Smyth (whose godfather discovered the first known asteroid), and Robert Menzies. Both men tended toward religious zealotry, and their observations and measurements of the Great Pyramid tended to get mixed in with their rather extreme religious beliefs. Much of the 'mystery' of the Great Pyramid is still the echo of their work.

The first proposition was that the pyramid is unique among the monuments of ancient Egypt, and that it was built from divine inspiration by a highly advanced race of invaders. Not only that but both the Biblical Israelites and the Anglo-Saxons – who, 'coincidentally', were the discoverers of the 'message' – were their descendants. It was proposed that the construction of the Great Pyramid encoded, within its various measurements, prophecies of future events, events which would form the basis of the Old Testament, the future history of Christianity, and the Second Coming of Christ. To pass on the message of the pyramid to future ages, it was built to certain precise mathematical proportions in order that it might attract attention and cause people to look further for the messages held within. This was done in part by embodying the

43

mathematical number *pi*, which is the ratio of the circumference of a circle to its radius. It is said that its measurements were obviously built around a high degree of astronomical knowledge and knowledge of the earth's surface.

Geometry

The modern and theologically dispassionate study of the Great Pyramid can be said to start with the great archaeologist Sir Flinders Petrie, who undertook the first precise measurements in 1880. A trained surveyor, his measurements were the best available until the invention of laser measuring devices. As the tourist season approached and Petrie had not yet finished his measurements, he took to going about the pyramid in nothing but his pink underwear – thereby keeping proper Victorian ladies and their escorts at a safe distance! His measurements were the first to determine with certainty that both the outer dimensions and those of the King's Chamber were built in a ratio of the diameter of a circle to its circumference, which is always slightly over 3.14, regardless of the size of the circle. This ratio is represented by the Greek letter *pi*.

In fact, both the Pyramid of the Sun in Mexico and the Great Pyramid are built to embody certain mathematical ratios related to *pi*. Mathematicians usually describe circles not in terms of the diameters, but of their radii. Since the radius of a circle is always half of its diameter, the ratio of the diameter to the circumference will always be 2 *pi*. These numbers were considered mystical by most ancient cultures, where the circle was in itself considered a sacred symbol. Thus every ancient structure that related to the circle, such as Stonehenge in the UK, required an effort on the part of its builders to determine, either mathematically or geometrically, this ratio. So it is with the construction of these two pyramids; but because the bases of pyramids are square rather than circular for the most part, the mathematical ratio set up was that of the height of the pyramid to the perimeter of its base – the sum of the length of its four sides. The Pyramid of the Sun is built in five distinct steps but is shorter than the Great Pyramid, although the area of its base

is virtually the same as the Great Pyramid's. The height of the Great Pyramid is related to the perimeter of its base in the ratio of exactly 2 *pi*; the height of the Pyramid of the Sun is in exactly the ratio of 4 *pi* with the perimeter of its base.

Not only is the Great Pyramid built to embody mathematical ratios, it is built to remarkable, if not unique, standards. The first construction feature notable about the Great Pyramid is the accuracy of the laying-out of its base. For such a huge structure (just over 225 metres along the edge of each side of the base on a side) there is less than 20 centimetres difference between its longest and shortest sides. The angular difference between the sides is a small fraction of a degree. Up until the invention of laser distance measuring equipment in the late 1970s, the layout of a modern building on this scale would not have matched this accuracy. The pyramid's base covers 13 acres, levelled to within a fraction of centimetre. More than 2½ million blocks of limestone and granite rise in 201 stepped layers to the height of a 40-storey building. Each of these blocks weighs from 2 to 70 tonnes. There is more stone here than in all the cathedrals and churches built in England since the beginning of the Christian era.

In Petrie's study of the casing stones, he found that they were square within a matter of a hundredth of a millimetre. Of this accuracy he remarked: 'Merely to place such stones in exact contact would be careful work, but to do so with cement in the joint seems impossible: it is to be compared with the finest optician's work on a scale of acres.' (*Secrets of the Great Pyramid*, Peter Tompkins).

Chambers and passages
of the Great Pyramid

Although its construction was well within the capabilities of Egyptians living at the time of Khufu, certain features of the Great Pyramid are mysterious. This is less from the standpoint of their construction, than of their function.

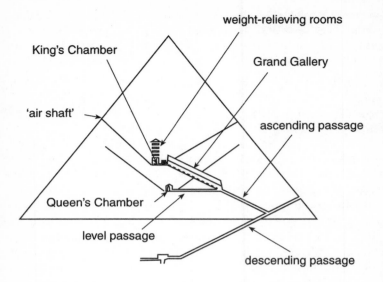

Section of the Great Pyramid showing the major structural components.

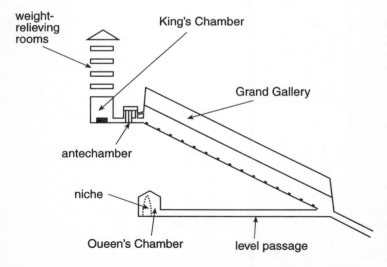

Diagram showing the chambers and passages of the Great Pyramid.

The current entrance to the Great Pyramid is through the irregular passage tunnelled into the pyramid by Arab treasure-seekers in the ninth century. But the original entrance was at the opening of the descending passage, framed by two huge limestone gables. The passage itself is remarkably small: 1 metre by 1.2 metres. It slopes downward at a fraction over a 26½-degree angle, almost precisely half of the 52-degree face angles of the pyramid as it descends 105 metres into the bedrock beneath the pyramid. It ends in a small, roughly hewn chamber which has been variously described as 'the original burial chamber' or, more simply, 'the pit'. The descending passage is remarkably straight, deviating over its 105-metre length by no more than a fraction of an centimetre.

The ascending passage is exactly the same dimensions as the descending passage, and rises at a small fraction over a 26-degree angle. At the upper end of its equally straight 39-metre length it enters the Grand Gallery. The Grand Gallery is by all standards the most remarkable single feature of the pyramid. The roof of the Gallery is corbelled – an arch-forming technique wherein the stones of each successive course project beyond those of the course below, giving an inverted stair-step effect. It is relatively uncommon in Egyptian architecture, but the Maya used it extensively. To make things as difficult as possible for the Egyptian engineers, the corbelled roof continues upward at the same 26-degree angle as the ascending passage. It is 2.3 metres wide at the base, and its walls rise 2.3 metres. Its corbels progress upward in seven steps to its full height of 8.4 metres, and the Gallery proceeds upward for 50 metres. Standing at the bottom of this chamber looking upward is as awe-inspiring as the pyramid itself.

Moving horizontally into the pyramid from the juncture of the ascending passage and the Grand Gallery, the level passage proceeds inward to the Queen's Chamber. Always regarded as unused, it measures just over 5.1 metres by 5.4 metres, with a gabled ceiling over 6 metres high. Its floor looks rough and unfinished. The eastern wall contains a niche 4.5 metres high, 1.5 metres wide, and originally just over 1 metre deep; it was deepened by Arab treasure-seekers looking for hidden chambers.

At the top of the Grand Gallery is the apparent focus of the entire pyramid: the King's Chamber. It is reached by crawling through a 1-metre high antechamber, apparently originally blocked with four granite portcullis-slabs. The chamber is a precise 2:1 rectangle, with its longest side just over 10.2 metres. The floor consists of 15 massive granite paving stones, and the walls are made of 100 huge granite blocks laid in five courses. Its ceiling consists of nine full-span granite blocks, each of which weighs upwards of 50 tonnes. Above the ceiling of the chamber in five tiers, are equally huge blocks described as 'relieving rooms', constructed to relieve the King's Chamber of the massive weight of the pyramid above. At the end of the King's Chamber is the stone box referred to as the Sarcophagus, allegedly that of the Pharaoh Khufu. Whether it is a sarcophagus at all is a matter of debate, as previous chapters have shown.

There are a few other features of the pyramid's interior, as the figures on page 46 show. Ascending from both the King's and Queen's Chambers or their vicinity are what have been described as 'air shafts'. What these were actually for is debatable, in that they never reached the outside of the pyramid, nor, in the Queen's Chamber, did they go all the way through the chamber walls either. They remained undiscovered until 1872. They are about 20 × 22 centimetres, and ascend steeply. One of them features in the further exploration of the pyramid described in the following chapter.

PYRAMIDOLOGY REVISITED

Returning to pyramidology, it was believed that within the pyramid, coded into its chambers and passages, was a 6,000-year-old prophetic history of the world. In the descending passage humanity was represented a decline towards ignorance and evil. Where it joins the ascending passage, Christ is born and leads humanity upwards toward the Light of the Grand Gallery, while the evil spirits continue on down the descending passage into the bowels of the earth. After taking the Great Step, humanity must kneel in submission as it passes through the low-roofed antechamber and into the King's Chamber,

wherein is experienced the Second Coming. The timescale was derived from the 'pyramid inch', with one pyramid inch per year since the creation of Adam – reflecting the even-then antiquated view that the world was created in 4004 BC – and continuing until the Second Coming. There was plenty more besides just this brief sketch.

As time passed and none of the pyramidologists' predictions based on the supposed encoding of prophecy within its structures happened, the whole idea became discredited. Prior to this even some academics were prepared to take it seriously, but in 1920, when the waters of the Mediterranean failed to turn to thick jelly and the rivers of the world failed to turn to blood as prophesied, it was the last gasp as far as academia was concerned.

As an amateur archaeologist with considerable experience remarked:

> *If a suitable unit of measurement is found... an exact equivalent to the distance of Timbuctu is certain to be found in the roof girder work of the Crystal Palace, or in the number of street lamps in Bond Street, or the specific gravity of mud, or the mean weight of adult goldfish.*

> (*Secrets of the Great Pyramid*, Peter Tompkins)

However whether or not the pyramidologists' interpretations are true there are some very definite modern discoveries that do point towards a 'pyramid power'. In the following chapters, we will explore some of these.

6

A MESSAGE FROM GIZA?

*D*epending *on which books you read, there are plenty of messages from Giza! In some versions, the Great Pyramid was built by extraterrestrials; in other versions the stones were floated into place using mystical devices like crystals. One can pick and choose as suits one's inclinations. But, there are several newer theories that deserve more serious consideration. These theories are presented in outline only because of available space, but the detail of the arguments may be read in full in the books in the Further Reading list at the back of the book.*

AN ORION CORRELATION?

In the 1980s Robert Bauval, a Belgian construction engineer with a strong interest in Egyptology and Egyptian stellar religion, noticed an apparent correlation in the sky with the layout of the Giza pyramids. In the constellation of Orion, three bright stars form the belt of the human figure: the lower two stars, Al Nitak and Al Nilam, are in perfect alignment with the diagonal of the belt, but the third and slightly smaller star Mintaka is slightly offset. This appears to be exactly the layout of the pyramids on the Giza plateau. The Great Pyramid and the similar-sized Pyramid of Kephren occupied the positions of the two brighter stars, while the smaller pyramid of Menkaure was offset in the same direction as the third and smallest star, Mintaka (*The Orion Mystery*, Bauval and Gilbert). But this seemed to fly in the face of archaeological orthodoxy, which held that Egyptian religion was based on sun worship, not on sky

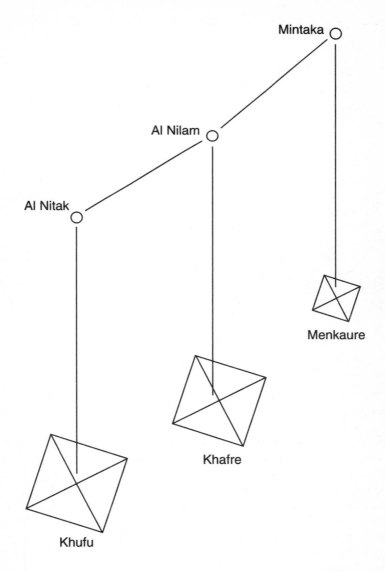

The three pyramids of Giza plotted against the three belt stars of the Orion constellation.

worship. But as Bauval and others pointed out, relatively few Egyptologists are equipped either by training or expertise to consider the problems of sky-associated religion, and its consequent expression in Egyptian architecture. But evidence has been there all along.

Modern indications increasingly suggest that the religion of the time was indeed star- and sky-based. This has important implications for the Pyramid Age. All previous interpretations of the pyramids – as well as the whole of Egyptian culture – have been based on the assumption that their roots existed in sun worship. There is no doubt that as the centuries passed this came to be true, and by the time the Greeks came to rule Egypt in the third century BC it was certainly true. However, serious doubt must now exist over whether this was true when the pyramids were built. As a consequence of Bauval's study, it now appears likely that the building of at least some of the other pyramids was directly connected to star positions and beliefs about the stars' religious meaning.

Belief in a sky-god or gods is also very likely to have been connected to a mysterious object called the *Ben-ben*. It was the most venerated object throughout, and quite possibly before, the Old Kingdom. The start of the worship of the Ben-ben is conventionally placed at 3100 BC – a date we will see is significant in later chapters. It rested atop a pedestal in its own temple in Heliopolis, the centre of Egyptian religion at that time, and now a suburb of modern Cairo. Heliopolis (from the Greek god of sun Helios) is a misleading name, in that it implies a solar religion was based there. Its ancient Egyptian name was Annu, meaning 'pillar', a reference to the rough-hewn stone pillar upon which the Ben-ben stood.

Egyptologists have long speculated that the Ben-ben was a meteorite, and even that it had a pyramidal shape, thus bestowing this shape with a special divine significance, as it had fallen from 'heaven'. The connection of meteorite impacts to religious belief is further explored in a later chapter. In combination, the pillar and pyramidal shape gave the shape of all future obelisks, and quite possibly, the shape of the pyramids themselves. Significant evidence of this is that the capstones of true pyramids were called Ben-bens.

Further, the Ben-ben was said to be made from *bja* metal, meaning 'metal from heaven'. That 'heaven' was associated with the sky is in itself significant. Most religions of the time were earth-centred, built around goddess figures representing nature – 'gods' were quite rare at the time of the Old Kingdom. The idea that early Egyptian religion was star-centred rather than sun-centred considerably shifts the emphasis of what is known about Egyptian religion. At its very heart was the god Osiris.

Osiris

Because he was connected with the most basic mysteries of life – death and resurrection – Osiris was the most significant of male Egyptian gods. Osiris may well claim to be the longest-worshipped god in the world. From the beginning of Egyptian civilization until the eradication of his cult by Christians in the fourth century AD, he was the primary god of the Egyptian pantheon. Early stories about him vary, but are concerned to various degrees with his relationship to other gods and goddesses of his time, and his death and resurrection. Although he was returned to life, he did not continue his life on earth, but became lord of the overworld – of heaven and the sky. The death and resurrection story of Jesus is a virtual copy of the Osiris story – possibly quite literally.

There is one very significant dimension to his story: the dead person is presented to Osiris after The Weighing of the Heart, the symbolic weighing of the person's life against *Ma'at*, the condition of being in the right-relationship with all creation. After their successful fulfillment of *Ma'at* the deceased actually *becomes* Osiris, or *an* Osiris, because his or her heart is pure. Their name after death becomes 'the Osiris...' followed by his or her name. Thus the pure become one with their god. The physical place where this occurred was *Sahu*, which correlates exactly to Orion, as we see below.

The connection of Orion with Osiris and the whole Egyptian philosophy of the afterlife is more than speculation. The Pyramid Texts clearly show several illustrations of the three stars of Orion's

belt in association with the path of the soul in the afterlife. Further, the three stars of Orion's belt are clear indicators as they rise above the horizon, that the rising of Sirius is not far behind. Thus the rising of Sirius was *the* major sacred event, and the rising of Orion as a precursor to the rise of Sirius had equally powerful spiritual connotations. The rise of Sirius correlated with the annual flooding of the Nile – an 'Osiris' event – and the 'rebirth' of Egypt each year. It must be made clear that the Egyptians did not call the star pattern Orion, but rather saw the three stars as part of a much larger human figure called Sahu. Sahu is depicted in a number of places, including the astronomical ceiling of Senmut's tomb, and is identified in the Pyramid Texts with Osiris (*Egyptian Astronomical Texts*, Neugebaure and Parker). Therefore the building of huge pyramids in connection with the celestial patterns at the very centre of Egyptian religious belief becomes perfectly logical.

Dow old is the Great Pyramid?

Other recent theories, particularly those of Graham Hancock, researcher into alternative interpretations of ancient history, and author of *The Fingerprints of the Gods*, place the building of the Giza 'Orion' pyramids in a much earlier age, thousands of years before the Pyramid Age. One thing is absolutely certain: either the Great Pyramid and/or other structures on the Giza plateau were built at roughly the time the Egyptologists claim, or they weren't. Both possibilities have important implications. If they were built in the Pyramid Age, then they can be considered as the best examples of pyramid-building of that age. If they were built at an earlier time, then when? Hancock suggests that Bauval's calculations place the positioning of the pyramids not around 2500 BC, but as Orion's belt looked around the year 10,450 BC. Further, he believes the pyramids to be evidence – among a mass of other evidence – that an advanced civilization existed at that time. This is certainly the time

frame others suggest for Atlantis, although it is not claimed that this civilization *was* Atlantis.

Related theories suggest that the various passageways of the Great Pyramid are oriented to specific stars, and most suggest the North Star was a major orienting point. But when trying to fix its age by the alignment of the stars with its passages, the problem always has been establishing which stars. The position of our sun and solar system, as well as irregularities in the earth's orbit and rotation when added to the actual movement of the stars themselves, create numerous problems for astronomical theories. Polaris, known today as the North Star, was not in its current position at the time the Great Pyramid was built. But which star was? It depends on when it was built, and which passage was intended to align with it. The descending passage is the most likely candidate, possibly oriented to the star Alpha Draconis, if it was built either around 2160 or 3440 BC, or Xi Mizar if it was built any time before 1500 BC.

Other evidence

There is other intriguing evidence that some of the constructions on the Giza necropolis are older than orthodox archaeology claims. This has been suggested by an American scholar, John Anthony West, whose research focused on two key structures: the Great Sphinx and the Valley Temple, a few hundred metres from the Sphinx. According to West, both of these structures showed clear signs of heavy erosion by water. This is significant in the case of the Sphinx in particular, in that it sits in a recess in a steep hillside, out of which it was carved from the living rock. This recess fills with sand very rapidly, and in dry desert conditions has had little opportunity to be weathered by the tiny amount of rainfall currently experienced at Giza. But, this has not always been so. The Sahara desert only began drying up at the end of the last Ice Age, and up to 12,000 years ago, or 10,000 BC, there would have been adequate rainfall to produce the weathering effects which have been observed. Further, Dr Robert Schoch, Professor of Geology at Boston

University, confirmed West's observations, which were in turn endorsed by almost 300 other geologists at the 1992 convention of the Geological Society of America (*Fingerprints of the Gods*, Graham Hancock).

A controversial discovery in the nineteenth century by French archaeologist Auguste Mariette may cast further light on the age of Giza. It is called the 'Inventory Stelae', an inscribed standing stone at the foot of the Sphinx, and on it are inscriptions stating that the Sphinx and the Giza pyramids were in existence long before the time of Khufu, and even at this time they were regarded as extremely ancient. They were reputed to have been built not by pharaohs, but to have come down from the 'First Time', when the gods supposedly first appeared on the earth. And, there is a suggestion that Kuhfu's Pyramid might actually be one of the three small pyramids alongside the Great Pyramid (*Ancient Egyptian Literature*, Miriam Lichthetim). Orthodox Egyptologists have rejected the Inventory Stelae as being of a hieroglyphic style too late for its claimed date of origin, yet as Hancock rightly points out, they readily accept the authenticity of a few highly dubious quarry marks when attributing the Great Pyramid to Khufu solely on the same basis.

A NEW CHAPTER

A new chapter opened in the story of the Great Pyramid in 1993. Because of the humidity build-up inside the pyramid, particularly in the King's Chamber, due to the large number of tourists entering the pyramid daily, the German Archaeological Institute in Cairo employed a German robotics engineer, Rudolf Gatenbrink, to use a small robot to clear out the ventilation shafts that rise from the King's and Queen's Chambers. He named his small robot Upuaut 2, after the ancient god, the Opener of the Ways. After successfully clearing the southern shaft of the King's Chamber, Upuaut was sent up the southern shaft of the Queen's Chamber. After a certain distance its television cameras showed the walls changing to fine Tura limestone, normally used for lining sacred precincts. At a further distance, Upuaut encountered a solid limestone door, with

metal fittings. Because of the door, it was unable to proceed further, raising the question: what is beyond the door? No one knows. But in 1997 the pyramid was closed for 'renovations'. Is this connected? No one is saying, and no information has thus far reached the public.

New theories and theorists

The new theories, not only about the origin of the Giza necropolis, but of the advanced nature of past and disappeared civilizations need to be taken seriously by the academic and archaeological establishments – if for no other reason than to disprove them. Academic and archaeological research does not exist in a vacuum. It is all funded either publicly or privately. If potentially important discoveries are being ignored because they don't fall within orthodox thought – which is often itself based on little more actual evidence than the newest theories – then the funders of that research have a right to ask: why? A remark by Nobel Prize-winning physicist Max Planck summarizes the obstacles facing the new theorists: 'A new scientific truth does not triumph by convincing its opponents and making them see the light, but rather because its opponents eventually die and a new generation grows up that is familiar with it.' We can only hope that this is not the case with these new theories, as they appear to hold within them – if true – major and important messages that may concern the survival of mankind itself.

7

AN EGYPTIAN CONNECTION?

As it appears that the Egyptian pyramids were the world's first, the question that must inevitably arise as to whether the idea of pyramids originated solely in Egypt and then spread elsewhere, or, whether it spontaneously arose in different places. The answer seems likely to be both.

As the belief grew that god lived in the sky, the idea of building a tall tower in order that humans could climb up and speak to him (gods who live in the sky are inevitably male gods in sky-god cultures) was a fairly natural extension of belief. Since no one knew how far away the sky was – most believed it to be no more than a few kilometres – getting 'closer' to god in order to make sure your requests to him and his messages to you got through, clearly made sense. The next logical stage was to build a series of short towers piled one on another and each slightly smaller than the one below it, in order to build a high structure that was still stable: a step-pyramid, in fact. The Bible records the building of such a structure for just that purpose: the tower of Babel. Other such structures also appeared in Mesopotamia, where they are referred to as ziggurats. These are, in fact, step-pyramids, as we saw in Chapter 2. Most of them were built some time after the Egyptian pyramids, so the idea could have come from Egypt. But, Mesopotamia was a long distance from Egypt, so the idea could have developed independently. There is currently no way to tell.

However, across the Atlantic, the pyramids of Mexico and Central America – collectively referred to as Mesoamerica – were built much later, and there is a considerable body of evidence to suggest that they may well have been inspired by Egypt.

BEARDED WHITE MEN

At the root of the evidence are numerous stories and legends of a mysterious teacher, described as a 'bearded white man', who brought civilization and advanced teaching to primitive peoples. These stories are nowhere more prevalent than in Mexico and in Central and South America. The Olmecs and Toltecs in Mexico, the Maya in Mesoamerica, and the Incas in Peru all developed spoken and written legends, and left ancient stone carvings clearly representing bearded Caucasians. Long predating the arrival of the Spanish, these have been found in several places. It is possible that the first Mesoamerican appearance of the mysterious Founder, as the 'bearded white man' is usually referred to, was in Olmec Mexico, in that it was the earliest culture to show evidence of the effects of his appearance. The Teotihuacan pyramids are other early evidence, although it may not have been the Olmecs who built them. The building of these pyramids is shrouded in almost as much mystery as the Giza pyramids.

Stories of the Founder passed down through the Olmecs to the Toltecs, who called him Quetzalcoatl, meaning 'Plumed Serpent', and finally to the Aztecs. Indeed, the Spanish conquest of the Aztecs was directly aided by these legends – Cortez and his men were believed to be the promised return of the 'bearded white god' Quetzalcoatl and his followers. Early stories of Quetzalcoatl, collected in Mexico by Spanish chroniclers, described him as 'a fair and ruddy-complexioned man with a long beard.' He was also spoken of as being 'a white man; a large man, broad browed, with huge eyes, long hair, and a great, rounded beard.' He 'condemned sacrifices, except of fruits and flowers, and was known as the god of peace... when addressed on the subject of war he is reported to have stopped up his ears with his fingers.' Another tradition of Quetzalcoatl is that he 'came from across the sea in a boat that moved by itself without paddles. He built houses and showed couples that they could live together as husband and wife; and since people often quarrelled in those days, he taught them to live in peace.' (Cited in *Atlantis; The Antidiluvian World*, Ignatius Donelly). He was reputed to be a healer who could cure by laying on hands,

and who revived the dead (*Mysteries of the Mexican Pyramids*, Peter Tompkins). In many respects this is a perfect description of the Egyptian god Horus, who was, among other things, the Egyptian god of healing.

According to some Maya texts, as many as 20 men came with the Founder: the sacred Maya calendar has months of 20 days, each named after a 'god'. The connection between the two is unproven, but quite likely. In the Maya version, they came from the east in boats and stayed for ten years. Their leader was Itzamna, meaning 'serpent of the east', a healer who could cure by laying on hands, and who revived the dead (*Mysteries of the Mexican Pyramids*, Peter Tompkins). Itzamna is the oldest god of the Maya, who has many of the characteristics of Quetzalcoatl, and is quite likely the same figure in early Maya form. He, and the 'gods' who arrived with him, are described by the Maya as wearing flowing robes, sandals, and having long beards and bare heads. Some of Itzamna's companions are described as being 'gods of fish', 'gods of agriculture', and a 'god of thunder' – 'gods' probably meaning in this case 'teachers'. He was believed to have introduced the knowledge of writing into Central America, to have brought the calendar, to have been a master builder, and was the father of mathematics, metallurgy and astronomy (*An Introduction to the Study of Maya Hieroglyphics*, Sylvanus Griswold Morley).

Egyptian clues

So, if there is an Egyptian connection, how did the Egyptians find their way to Mesoamerica from the other side of the Atlantic? A strong clue is that the 'bearded white men' were said to have arrived in a 'boat made of snakes', a perfect description of a reed boat, with its undulations in the waves appearing as the writhing of snakes. The boat was 'moving without paddles' which is possible with a sail, something that could well have been a mystery to people who had not yet discovered it. Large reed boats perfectly capable of cross-ocean

navigation – as Thor Heyerdahl proved with the Ra expeditions in the 1960s, when he sailed a reed boat across the Atlantic. Such boats were in use in civilizations around the Mediterranean and Nile long before 2000 BC, and well before the supposed founding of the Olmec culture. As previous chapters have shown, the Egyptians were perfectly aware of the movements of the stars in the night sky, and star-navigation was certainly possible at the time. So, getting to Mesoamerica was well within Egyptian capabilities. But why would they have gone there in the first place?

Egypt has been an expanding empire at various times in its history. Although generally insular, evidence of far-flung trading posts is sprinkled through much of northeast Africa, Palestine, and Mesopotamia. Contact with the New World could have been nothing more than a trading expedition. However, there is a more likely possibility: they were fleeing from the upheavals at the collapse of the Old Kingdom, when Egypt came under the heel of the Hyskos. Significantly, at a time when the Pyramid Age was nearly over in Egypt, it was just beginning in Mesoamerica.

Evidence from the calendar

Almost uniquely among ancient peoples, both the Egyptians and Olmecs (and later the Maya, who inherited the knowledge from the Olmecs) possessed the knowledge that the earth's year is just over 365 days. While differing in the number of months, each have a basic 360-day period plus five extra days. In the Western world, we didn't develop a calendar as accurate until just a few centuries ago. How did two cultures an ocean apart gain such accuracy? There is another mystery here: the earliest archaeological evidence for the Olmec civilization starts about 2000 BC. So, why did the Olmecs use a calendar that began in 3114 BC, a date that corresponds almost exactly with the date of the founding of the Egyptian Old Kingdom?

Mythological similarities

Another important piece of evidence about an Olmec/Maya/Egyptian connection is the distinct similarity between the mythologies of both the Egyptians and the Maya. In ancient times it was the fashion to cast spiritual revelations in stories of mythology, presented in the form of metaphors or allegories. We can be certain that when the metaphors or allegories, which are different for each culture, are similar, then the fundamental understandings of life and the universe will be also. What both mythologies demonstrate is a mutual understanding of the essential duality of life: up/down; hot/cold; good/ evil; life/death; underworld/overworld.

In Egyptian mythology, Isis and her husband Osiris were twins, born from the goddess Nut, an incarnation of Mother Nature. Their younger brother and sister, Seth and Nephtys, were also twins, born likewise from Nut. One night Osiris mistakenly made love to Nephtys, thinking she was Isis. From that mistaken union, Osiris's oldest son, Anubis, was born. Nephtys's husband Seth wasn't at all pleased with this event, and killed his elder brother, Osiris. Osiris's sarcophagus floated down the Nile, and was washed up on a beach in faraway Syria (an Egyptian metaphor for 'the back end of nowhere', the equivalent of the Maya Underworld). Isis took on human form and went to Syria to retrieve Osiris's body. She has relations with Osiris's body, and conceives Horus. The allegory here suggests that 'out of death comes life'. Osiris became a resurrection figure in Egyptian mythology; the rebirth/resurrection of the Nile in its annual inundation was believed to be a function of the resurrection of Osiris. It was signalled by the rising of Sirius.

In Maya mythology – which has equivalents in other Mesoamerican mythologies – twin sons are also born, One-Hunahpu and Seven-Hunahpu, and together with the daughter of the lord of the underworld, Blood Gatherer, they in turn give birth to twin sons, jointly fathered. The sons are Hunahpu and Xbalanque. Hunahpu and Xbalanque go through a series of adventures in the underworld, an archetypal hero-quest like that embodied by Isis. One-Hunahpu and Seven-Hunahpu have likewise undergone a series of trials and

initiations in the underworld, culminating with the overthrow of the Lords of Death. Death and resurrection play a major part in their story, and they become resurrection figures like Osiris and Horus.

Now it must be said that similarities in mythologies does not necessarily mean that one came from the other, but it is also true that there is enough similarity equally to speculate on a common source.

The Popol Vuh

The ancient Maya book, the *Popol Vuh*, records the legend of the great quest undertaken by three intrepid Maya nobles who 'journeyed to the east', and 'passed over the sea' to reach the centre of all Mesoamerican civilization – Tula – to 'receive lordship'. The lord of the east, named Nacxit was described as 'the great lord and sole judge over a populous domain'. During their stay they were given emblems of kingship and were educated. They 'brought back the writing of Tulan, the writing of Zuyua [sounding similar to 'Libya', the ancient Egyptian name for 'Egypt'], and they spoke of their investiture in their signs and in their words'. When these nobles returned, they resumed their lordship over their tribes. At the times of their deaths 'their faces did not die; they passed them on' – a possible reference to Egyptian-style death masks, which appear in Maya entombments. Whether they actually went to Egypt or if they did indeed go to Olmec Tula, the use of Egyptian-sounding names and Egyptian cultural symbols could easily have been part of the Olmec culture.

There is one possibility that does not seem to have been considered by archaeological orthodoxy: that the Olmecs may have been Egyptians, exiles from the collapsed Old Kingdom. Not a single Olmec skeleton has been found, and there is not a single shred of evidence to say that the Olmecs were Mesoamericans. Evidence that they just might have been Egyptians is found further south.

The Cloud People

Recent discoveries in Peru have cast a whole new light on the question of the 'bearded white men'. Explorer Gene Savoy discovered extensive ruins in the high mountains of northern Peru, in an area said by the Incas at the time of the Spanish conquest to be the home of people whom they called 'Cloud People'. The Incas told Spanish chroniclers that they had only conquered the Cloud People in the 1480s, just a century before the arrival of the Spanish.

The Incas described them as 'beautiful people', tall, blue-eyed, blonde and white-skinned, who lived in seven great cities in the Chachapoyas area of the Andes. While the Spanish dismissed the Inca claims, Gene Savoy wasn't so sure. Starting in the 1970s he made several expeditions to the Chachapoyas area. In the vicinity of the Lake of the Condors, he made an exciting discovery: a huge, ancient city with nearby cliff-tombs, unknown elsewhere in South America. In these were discovered the mummies of tall, white people. They were embalmed in a way never seen in South America before, in a way similar to Egyptian mummies: the skin had been treated with an as yet unknown substance to prevent decay in the humid jungle, and the internal organs had been removed. Savoy believes that it is entirely possible that boats from Egypt or Mesopotamia could have arrived from across the Atlantic, and sailed up the Amazon to within relatively easy distance of Chachapoyas ('Secrets of the Cloud People', QED, 1998).

There is a footnote to the Quetzecoatl/Itzamna story. After living with the native peoples and teaching them their skills, Quetzecoatl and his followers were defeated in battle by a local chieftain called Smoking Mirror. They then sailed away towards the east, never to return. Perhaps they went to Peru.

8 INDUCEMENTS OF THE GODS?

In an earlier chapter we explored some of the 'uses' of pyramids. One that was mentioned was that they were built as part of an overall strategy to communicate to the gods, and to induce them to either undertake, or to cease undertaking, some particular activity – this is the basis of prayer even in the modern world, after all. Because the pyramids were such a massive endeavour, involving whole communities, both in time and resources, the reason for their construction must have been compelling, and the community must have derived some benefit from the gods through their activity in constructing the pyramid. But perhaps the compulsion was even stronger than that. Perhaps the need to influence the gods was particularly strong. But what might that need have been? Very possibly it may have been to induce the gods to stop dropping civilization-ending burning mountains from the sky.

ASTEROIDS, COMETS, AND METEORITES

Comets have been seen by most cultures as omens of doom throughout history, and this has generally been dismissed as superstition. However, there is growing evidence that the impact of both comet fragments and asteroids have had a much larger influence on the development and/or the decline of human civilizations than previously thought. Comets used to be thought of as 'dirty snowballs', but are now recognized to be large accumulations of rock and other

solid matter that have the capability to fragment and shower our planet with pieces – meteorites. That the dinosaurs were wiped out by the impact of a huge asteroid, a large stone or metal piece from a planet that broke up between Mars and Jupiter, is now an accepted theory. The effect of such impacts on human civilization has been largely ignored until very recently, when startling evidence began to emerge. Studies of tree rings from around the world have revealed that the planet suddenly cooled between 2354 BC and 2345 BC, and archaeologists excavating in northern Syria have discovered that at the same time a catastrophic event caused the mud-brick buildings of that area to disintegrate. Other researchers in the Middle East have found soil layers from around 2400 BC containing traces of minerals only found in meteorites. Other evidence suggests that much earlier impacts brought to an end the last Ice Age, and other equally dramatic climatic changes.

An astronomer at Armagh Observatory, Dr Bill Napier, believes that around the year 2350 BC, a large comet broke up near the earth, and the impact of some of its fragments ultimately brought to an end several ancient civilizations. Within relatively few years of around 2350 BC, the Egyptian Old Kingdom, the Sumerian civilization in Mesopotamia, and the Harrapin civilization of the Indus Valley in India all severely declined and collapsed.

We have already examined evidence that the entire spate of pyramid-building in Egypt sprang from the fall of the Ben-ben, which fell some centuries before 2350 BC, and was venerated throughout the whole period of the Old Kingdom. Indeed, it may have been part of a fall that occurred before 3200 BC, which, if Hancock is correct, ended whatever civilization preceded the Egyptians and the Sumerians.

WRITTEN EVIDENCE

There is certainly no lack of ancient records that describe events which sound like comet or meteor falls. References to fires from the sky appear in most cultures, myths and religions, many of which involve winged serpents battling in the sky before one crashes to

earth. Indeed, the original 'Feathered Serpent', widespread throughout Mesoamerica, may be just such a 'creature': the comet's head can certainly take a 'feathered' appearance, and the tail can be sinuous like a serpent. In the New Testament, the Book of Revelation describes a huge burning mountain falling from the sky, dropping hail and fire on the earth while the sun and moon are darkened. In the Old Testament we find the well-known story of Sodom and Gomorrah, destroyed by a rain of fire and brimstone from the skies. Nearby, fireballs in the sky appear frequently in Babylonian astrology. The Book of Exodus records: 'there was hail, and fire mingled with hail ... there was none like it in all the land of Egypt since it became a nation ... and the hail smote every herb of the field, and broke every tree of the field.' Indeed, this may record the same event that destroyed Sodom and Gomorra. More than that, it may be a record of the 2350 BC event.

Egyptian pyramid evidence

Another of the mysteries of the Giza plateau, is that the two largest pyramids appear to have been built in two separate stages. Both were started and construction was abandoned for some reason, to be taken up again at a much later time. The evidence is in the construction of the pyramids themselves. Both pyramids are built from a number of separate courses of limestone blocks, and engineering logic and common sense would dictate that the blocks should get smaller as they go toward the top – especially given that the larger blocks can weigh ten to fifteen tonnes each. And in the Great Pyramid, the first 18 courses of blocks did diminish in size: until course 18 the blocks only weigh a 'few' tonnes each. But, at the 19th course the blocks suddenly get much larger again, having been raised more than 30 metres into the air at this stage. Why?

The second largest pyramid, that attributed to Kephren, follows a slightly different but equally noticeable construction: the first few courses are built of massive limestone blocks, up to 1.8 metres thick and 6 metres in length. Above that, the pyramid is built of 'normal' sized blocks. This begs the question, were the first constructions on

the Giza plateau not pyramids at all, but platforms? The Mayan and Mexican pyramids serve exclusively as temple platforms: was this perhaps the case initially at Giza? If so, what precipitated their conversion into pyramids? Was it a comet, or the threat of an impact?

There is a further piece of evidence. One of the pyramids at Dashur shows signs of hasty completion. Up to a certain level the construction is first-rate; above that it is virtually thrown together, and has seriously deteriorated. Was this connected to the impact event?

WORLDWIDE EVIDENCE

If there was nothing more than what has just been described, the connection of pyramid-building to catastrophic astronomical events would be tenuous. But there is much, much more.

Beginning in roughly 2500 BC, and corresponding closely to Dr Napier's discoveries, there was a general shift from earth goddess religions, those which saw the earth and nature itself as the governing deity, to the idea of a male deity living in the sky, wrathful and meting out terrible justice to those who upset him. This is the time when intense astronomical observations were being made across much of the world: Sumerians, Egyptians, Babylonians, Chinese, and the builders of Stonehenge in England, all began to make accurate surveys of the sky, and entire civilizations began to be based on astrology – that is, on what was observed in the sky. The tower of Babel was built so men could climb up and speak to God, and in other places in the world standing stones were erected to delineate the summer solstice – Stonehenge was built as a kind of astronomical computer. So, why was there a sudden and intense interest in the sky?

There are a number of beliefs around the world that the planet goes through cycles of catastrophic destructions. Buddhist scriptures speak in terms of 'Suns', of which there are believed to be seven; each of these is doomed to come to an end by water, fire, or wind. We are currently in the Seventh Sun at the end of which 'the earth will break into flames'. In China, is there the belief that the earth

has gone through a series of cyclic destructions: each of the perished ages are called *Kis*, ten of which are said to have elapsed up until the time of Confucius. At the end of each Kis 'in a great convulsion of nature, the sea is carried out of its bed, mountains spring up out of the ground, rivers change course, human beings and everything are ruined, and the ancient traces effaced...' (*An Historical and Disruptive Account of China*, Murray, Crawford *et al*.)

There is a reference in the Bible, in Peter 2:3, that discusses the last days in apocalyptic terms that sound like an impact event:

> *We must be careful to remember that during the last days there are bound to be people who will be scornful and (who will say), everything goes on as it has since it began at the creation. They are choosing to forget that there were heavens at the beginning and that the earth was formed by the word of God out of water and between the waters, so that the world of that time was destroyed by being flooded by water. By the same word, the present sky and earth are destined for fire ... the Day of the Lord will come as a thief in the night, and then with a war the sky will vanish, the elements will catch fire and fall apart, and the earth and all it contains will be burned up.*

In Hinduism, on the broadest scale of things is the Day of Bhrama, a cyclic time span spreading over millions of years. On a smaller time scale, Hindus believe that we are living in the age called Kali Yuga, which is the last and most chaotic age of mankind. According to Indian astrologers, the Kali Yuga began in 3100 BC, a date corresponding almost exactly to the founding of the Old Kingdom, the beginning of the Olmec/ Maya calendar, and the beginning of the current Maya Fifth Sun.

The Maya Five Suns

The Maya record in their sacred book, the *Popol Vuh*, what may be the most accurate description preserved of an impact event. They, along with other Mesoamerican peoples, believe that in the past several thousand years, the world has gone through four periods,

called 'Suns', of catastrophic destruction and rebuilding. We are now in the Fifth Sun, a period which is soon to end. The description of what happened in one such catastrophe is entirely consistent with an impact event:

> *They were pounded down to the bones and tendons, smashed and pulverized, even to the bones. The earth was blackened because of this; the black rainstorm began, rain all day and rain all night.*
>
> *The stones, their hearth stones were shooting out, coming right out of the fire.*
>
> *They want to climb up on the houses, but they fall as the houses collapse.*
>
> *They want to climb the trees; they're thrown off by the trees.*
>
> *They want to get inside caves, but the caves slam shut in their faces.*
>
> *The sky – earth was already there, but the face of the sun – moon was clouded over. There came a rain of resin from the sky.*
>
> The Popol Vuh, trans. Dennis Tedlock

Here we see the immediate result of the impact: the violent shaking from the impact itself – the hearth stones shooting out and the collapse of houses; the rain of fire and resin (petroleum by-products released by the heat of the impact); the darkening of the sun and moon from impact debris; the fall of hail from moisture hurled high into the atmosphere to freeze before falling back. And the subsequent cooling of the region from 'nuclear-winter' type effects. The *Popol Vuh* recounts a time when the Maya experienced a time of intense cold: 'And so again the tribes arrived, again done in by the cold. Thick were the white hail, the blackening storm, and white crystals. The cold was incalculable. They were simply overwhelmed.' References to highly unusual cold appear in connection with similar sounding events in the Bible and such events would have been totally unheard of tropical Yucatan.

In its record of the ending of past Suns, the *Popol Vuh* gives us a rough timescale:

The First Sun, Matlactli Atl: duration 4008 years. The First Sun was destroyed by water in the sign matlactli atl [ten water]. It was called apachiohualiztli [flood, deluge]... Some say that only one couple escaped, protected by an old tree living near the water. Others say that there were seven couples who hid in a cave until the flood was over and the waters had gone down. They re-populated the earth and were worshipped as gods in their nations. . .

Second Sun, Ehecoatl: duration 4010 years. This Sun was destroyed by ehecoatl [wind serpent]... one man and one woman, standing on a rock, were saved from destruction . . .

Third Sun, Tleyquiyahuillo: duration 4081 years. This Sun was destroyed by fire. . .

Fourth Sun, Tzontlilic: duration 5026 years. Men died of starvation after a deluge of flood and fire. . .

Clearly the dates of the Maya Suns predate the Pyramid Age in Egypt. But if, as speculated upon in the last chapter, the idea of pyramids arrived in Mesoamerica from Egypt, might not the idea have arrived also that pyramids were a way of warding off such catastrophes? Might this not explain the explosion of pyramid-building in Mesoamerica? This is just speculation, but, speculation grounded in solid evidence.

OTHER EVIDENCE

Curiously, the site in South America producing the most dramatic physical evidence of what may be an impact event is also the place where the only South American pyramid has been found: the city of Tiahuanaco, on the shores of Lake Titicaca, in Peru. Tiahuanaco presents one of the great mysteries of modern archaeology. Few archaeologists can agree on a date for its founding: estimates vary from 2000 BC or even earlier, to the ninth century AD. Whoever built this city, and whenever they built it, it contains an even greater mystery than the date of its founding. In 1945, archaeologist Arthur Posansky discovered evidence of a catastrophic event at Tiahuanaco.

A combination of flood and earthquake was needed to produce the evidence he found: '...chaotic disorder among wrought stones, utensils, tools, and an endless variety of other things. All of this had been moved, broken, and accumulated in a confused heap.' Mixed among the debris were human remains, and the remains of lake-dwelling shells and fish. 'Layers of alluvium [water-laid sand and gravel] cover the whole field of ruins, and lacusterine [lake-originated] sand mixed with shells from Titicaca... accumulated in places surrounded by walls...' (*Fingerprints of the Gods*, Graham Hancock). What caused this deposit, and why was there such violence? Was it caused by an earthquake? Or by the violent shaking of the ground from a nearby meteor impact? Evidence for this may be found further south in Argentina, where a chain of small impact craters dating from around 2900 BC has been discovered along an 18-kilometre track. Although this is over two thousand kilometres from Lake Titicaca, there is no reason to assume that if a number of objects fell at the same time, it was only those whose craters have been found; other, larger objects may well have fallen further north, both near Lake Titicaca and in Maya Yucatan. Equally, the date of the fall could easily be closer to 3100 BC, and could even have been part of a wider fall, some of which may have landed in the Old World. There is further evidence that the Titicaca flood was caused by an impact: the climate in the Titicaca region underwent a serious change after the catastrophic event that destroyed the city. It became colder, and archaeological evidence shows that the survivors, after a struggle to adapt and survive, eventually moved off to better climes. This may be the same 'time of cold' recorded in the *Popol Vuh*. There is also evidence that a meteorite was worshipped in the ancient Andes. One of the titles the Incas gave to Viracocha, the South American equivalent of Quetzalcoatl, was Illa-Tika. This is translated as 'original thunderstone', and may indeed have been a meteorite (*The Secret of the Incas*, William Sullivan).

Given that the pyramid shape itself may result from the shape of a meteorite, the Ben-ben, thus connecting the shape to potentially disastrous celestial events, it may just be possible that many of the world's pyramids were built to deliver one message to God, in their various ways: please don't do it again.

INSIDE THE PYRAMID

The first indication that unusual and as yet unidentified forces are at work inside pyramids is usually attributed to a French man, Maurice Bovis. He apparently noticed a rubbish container in the King's Chamber which contained the corpses of dead cats and other small animals that had wandered into the pyramid and died. He noticed that there was no smell and no decay – the bodies were dry and mummified despite the high humidity in the chamber. He wondered if the pyramid itself could have been responsible for this. He made a wooden model of the pyramid, 0.9 metres along each edge of the base, and oriented north. He placed a dead cat inside in a position equivalent to the position of those found in the King's Chamber – a third of the way up from the base. Three days later it was dessicated and free of decay – in other words, mummified. Other organic materials were experimented with, including several that decay quickly, with the same results.

Karyl Drbal, a Czech radio engineer, heard of Bovis's experiments, and conducted experiments of his own, coming to be conclusion that the pyramid shape had a definite effect on the chemical and biological processes that take place within it. He eventually patented a famous – and much derided – cardboard pyramid, within which he claimed razor blades would recrystallize and resharpen themselves.

Other theorists have suggested that the pyramid shape, and in particular the Great Pyramid shape, sets up resonances in the various fields of energy – cosmic rays, electrical discharges, gravity waves, and so on – that envelop the earth. And that these resonances, both of known and yet to be discovered energy, are

what create the 'pyramid effect'. Recent discoveries have indirectly cast new light on this possibility.

Questions have inevitably arisen about the presence of yet undiscovered chambers within the Great Pyramid. There are a number of stories and legends from antiquity, but thus far they have proven to be no more than just that. But there is still a persistent idea among archaeologists and pyramidologists alike that there is more to be discovered. There is certainly plenty of room: only a tiny fraction of the bulk of the pyramid is occupied by its known chambers and passages. One clue may be the large numbers of black diorite chips discovered among the debris from the building of the pyramid. Thus far no diorite has been found lining chambers anywhere within. It is possible that since it was a popular stone for statuary, the chippings resulted from work on a large statue that has since been removed, but an additional chamber certainly cannot be ruled out. In fact, these stories eventually led to the first real 'scientific' exploration within a pyramid.

The search for additional chambers landed squarely in the realm of science in the late 1960s, when Nobel Prize-winner Dr Luis Alverez developed a means of measuring the passage of cosmic rays. When placed in a pyramid, a monitor recorded the passage of the rays, which lose part of their energy as they move through an object. Where a chamber exists, the rays will be less affected, and by taking readings in several positions, its presence can be triangulated. The first trial use of the device was in the Kephren's Pyramid, situated next to the Great Pyramid, and built at the same angles. Because Kephren was the son of the supposed builder of the Great Pyramid, Alvarez assumed that some of the ideas of Khufu's architects for hiding chambers would not have been used, and therefore his son's pyramid might well have incorporated them. Kephren's Pyramid has no known internal chambers like the Great Pyramid, with the exception of a 'burial chamber' just at its base, thus the possibility of undiscovered chambers seemed greater.

After two million measurements, the results were submitted to computer analysis. Nothing was discovered. Or was it? An Egyptian colleague who ran an independent computer analysis of the data in Egypt was reported to have said that different patterns emerged at each

computer run, and that as far as he was concerned there were forces at work in the pyramid which defied the laws of physics. Although Alvarez later repudiated the statement, questions still remain.

Indeed, there are many unanswered questions that can be loosely categorized under the heading of 'pyramid power'. We are only just beginning to discover the complex range of electromagnetic, gravitational and radiation influences that human life is both subjected to, and evolved within. That pyramids can effect those fields is not only possible, but in some instances, proven. Electromagnetic fields and their effects on the human body are only just beginning to be understood. Some of the earliest discoveries were made in 1952 by a German scientist, W.O. Schumann. He identified waves of very low frequency associated with the earth's own magnetic and electrical field. Schumann waves, as they are known, pulse almost within the same frequency range as brainwaves between 1 and 30 Hz.

Schumann suggested that these waves may influence all life, but the implications of this go far beyond that: life evolving on the earth must, of necessity, have evolved in harmony with these waves. Later research has shown that these waves are generated between the inner and outer core of the earth. Because the inner core is solid and the outer core is molten, 'slippage' occurs between the outer part of the earth and the inner core as the earth rotates. This acts as a dynamo, generating not only the earth's magnetic field, but the other energies as well. Important evidence for this and the earth's wave effects came from some of the first manned spaceflights – flights at a distance from the earth where the wave effects were very much reduced. Astronauts returned from space feeling distressed and disorientated until devices for generating Schumann waves were installed in the spacecraft.

Jet lag may be in part related, coming about as a result of being shielded by the plane's metallic casing, and flying at an altitude where Schumann waves are considerably weaker. It is usually made worse by moving to a place where the waves are pulsing at a different point in their 24-hour rhythm, reflected in the variations in the electromagnetic field of the earth from place to place. As with cosmic rays, other energetic features of the planet's total energy field

are affected by bulky objects, such as mountains – and pyramids. The presence of pyramid-sized objects is enough to register gravity-field effects on a gravitometer, for example. In common with measurements taken inside caves and mineshafts, there is a definite shielding effect as one goes deeper underground. It is highly likely that such waves would be blocked or modified, or both, by the bulk and geometry of pyramids. One often reported experience inside the Great Pyramid is that the rules of time/space on the inside are somehow different than on the outside. When the geometry of the pyramid is combined with the shielding effect of its bulk, that the natural energy environs outside of the pyramid would be modified to some degree is a certainty. The forces involved may or may not all be measurable to science, but then many of the most important still are not even known, much less measurable.

An example of a totally unidentified energy that directly affects us, but is only measurable indirectly, is one which is likely to be blocked or altered by pyramids. Its discovery came from a Japanese physician, Maki Takata, who discovered that the flocculation index (a measure of blood's clotting rate) varies throughout the day, becoming very low at night and suddenly rising rapidly as morning approaches. It varies directly both with sunrise and with the appearance of sunspots. The index rise actually begins before sunrise as if the blood 'knows' that sunrise is coming. To test that the rise is directly related to the blood's 'sensing' the rising sun, several people were taken to places where a full eclipse of the sun was to take place, a place where whatever solar effects there might be would be blocked out by the moon. As predicted, as the eclipse progressed the flocculation index dropped, rising again as the eclipse ended. It is still totally unknown which solar radiation produces the effect, or how the blood senses it, but it is powerful enough to penetrate almost everything except the moon. And, obviously, the earth itself, in that the index drops during the hours of darkness when the sun is behind the earth. The effect has been observed everywhere where tests have been carried out, except one that was done deep underground in a mine! (*The Cosmic Clocks*, Michel Gauquelin.) One place it hasn't been tried yet is inside a pyramid, but the outcome of it is likely to surprise no one.

Aside from the more esoteric interpretations of what goes on inside pyramids, there are very real and identifiable effects, and when we realize that we have yet to discover many of the energies that affect our lives and the world around us, it should come as no surprise whatever that pyramids will alter them as well. When science is ready to look for them, within and around the pyramids just might be a good place to start looking.

10

YOUR OWN
PYRAMID

*T*he subject of pyramids has fascinated us for centuries. Only
relatively recently, with the discovery of 'pyramid power', have
people from all walks of life begun to obtain personal pyramids for the
purpose of experimentation, or to use their 'powers'.

When it comes to acquiring personal pyramids, there are basically
two options: buy or build. We will look at the 'buy' option first. The
most popular pyramids are those made of glass or crystal, and range
in size from about a centimetre to several centimetres measured
along the edge of the base. There are several considerations when
buying a pyramid of this type: first, the distinction between crystal
and 'crystal'. A large portion of the totally transparent and
multicoloured 'crystals' are actually a type of glass. Many people
will purchase these thinking that they are buying a natural stone
pyramid, or at least one that has the characteristics of natural stone.
The word 'crystal' is misnomer when it is applied to glass: the very
definition of 'glass' is that it has no internal structure – it is in fact, a
very thick liquid. 'Crystal' as it applies to natural stone, implies a
very precise and highly ordered arrangement of its internal
constituents. Thus they are exact opposites of each other and will
have very different characteristics. Specifically what those
characteristics are is impossible to say, because with each individual
piece there are many variable combinations of internal structure,
external finish, and actual geometry of the pyramid itself.

Many reckon that the most energetically active pyramids are those
in which the faces are cut at the same angles relative to the base as
those of the Great Pyramid. This angle is very close to 52 degrees: it

is as close as you will be able to measure it in a small pyramid. In glass pyramids and natural stone pyramids, the shapers of those pyramids are often much more interested in conserving the materials they are using than in trying to reach any sort of precise geometric configuration. Thus relatively few of the pyramids you will be offered at your local pyramid store will actually have Great Pyramid proportions. Below is a gauge which can be transferred onto cardboard or some other material, that is set at precisely 52 degrees. If you desire a pyramid cut at those angles, just cut out the 'vee' of the angle and take this with you when you go pyramid shopping!

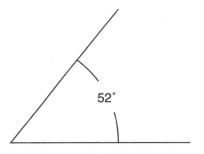

Base angle gauge.

So, is there anything to choose between glass pyramids and natural stone pyramids? The answer has to be yes, but in that we cannot precisely define 'pyramid power' in huge pyramids, neither can we define it in small ones. Nonetheless, there will be some instinctive reaction that each purchaser will have to the pyramids offered to him or her, which will in some way intuitively indicate which one is the 'correct' one.

Other types of ready-made pyramids are also offered for sale, commonly made from sheet metal. Copper seems to be a favourite material for the manufacture of these, although pyramids made of other metals, or wood or plastic, do appear from time to time.

On a somewhat larger scale, are the 'meditation' pyramids, which usually consist of nothing more than a frame of connected rods which, when assembled, is large enough for one person to sit inside.

It is alleged that the effects of simply creating an outline of the pyramid are the same as if a solid pyramid were actually there. All of the preceding types of pyramids can be purchased from outlets specializing in esoteric and New Age subjects.

The next option is to build your own. The only limitation here is your own imagination – and space! Small pyramids for experimental purposes can be made from cardboard or other readily available household materials, or you can buy materials from your local DIY store. Pyramids large enough to seat several people can be built in your back garden from any number of materials – but check your local planning regulations before you start. If you decide to build your own pyramid, you will need to know its proportions. The easiest method is to lay out four triangular sides of the correct dimensions, and then assemble them. This method works whether you are making a small pyramid from cardboard, or a larger one from plywood or other materials. For an open-framework pyramid a slightly different method is suggested in later paragraphs. It is recommended you work in metric measurement, because it simplifies the necessary calculations. Don't be put off by the mathematics – it couldn't be easier.

You will need to construct four triangles whose sides are in the ratios shown below. For pyramids only a few centimetres high, the diagonal length ratio of 1.17 is close enough; for larger pyramids like that described below, 1.176 will come even closer. To make things easy, use a whole number of centimetres or millimetres for the

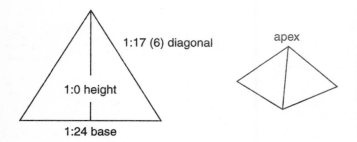

Ratios of side lengths for building a pyramid to Great Pyramid proportions.

height of the triangle, and the other two sides fall easily into place. If you decide to build a larger, garden-sized pyramid, remember that the actual height of the finished pyramid will be less than the height of the triangular face by roughly 15 per cent, because the faces are tilted inward to come together at the apex. So, if you build your garden pyramid with a triangle height of 2 metres, the apex height will be about 1.7 metres.

To lay out your four triangles, they will be 2 metres high, the length of the base will be 1.24 × 2 metres, or 2.48 metres, and the length of the diagonals will be 1.176 × 2 metres, or 2.352 metres. If this was a small cardboard pyramid, you would now be ready to assemble the faces. But in a larger pyramid the thickness of the material must be taken into account. If you attempt to assemble them without taking this into account, then it is impossible to fit them together correctly, as shown below (a). There are three basic options for fitting the faces: bevel the edges (b), overlap just one edge of each face (c), or overlap alternate faces (d). Depending on your skills and the materials you are using, all three will work well. Option b requires considerable skill and proper equipment. Options c and d are much easier. All that is necessary in c is to mark off along the right edge of

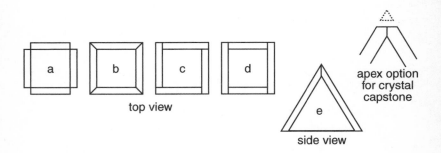

Pyramid assembly options.

each triangle, the thickness of the material. Be sure to do it along the same edge for each (or you can use the left edge if you wish as long as you use the same edge all around). Do this step before cutting out the pieces! Option d requires you to take the thickness amount off both edges of two opposite faces, to get an overlap as shown in e. This might be preferred so that two of the faces show no overlap. Some bevelling just at the apex will be necessary in c and d, as shown at the top in e. Do a trial assembly before the final assembly, and cut the bevels to fit then – it is much easier than trying to work them out beforehand. Using the proportions shown, your finished pyramid will be in exact Great Pyramid proportions.

Open-frame pyramids are even easier to build. They can be made from metal tubing or even bamboo canes. For one of these you only need to lay out two triangles. Joining the corners is a bit trickier, but it can be done simply by cutting out small triangles of thin plywood for each corner, and just gluing the framing onto them. If you are using wooden doweling or bamboo canes, flatten the side with a file or knife where it is to be glued for a stronger joint. After building the two sides, just stand them point to point at the apex, and connect the corners of their two bases with two other base-length pieces, as shown below. Use plywood triangles at the corners of the base pieces and the apex as with the assembly of the two sides.

If you intend to place a crystal pyramid at the apex of your pyramid,

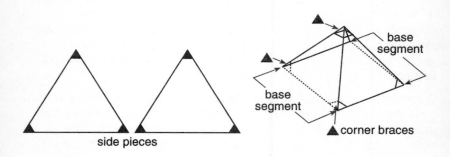

Assembly of an open-frame pyramid.

whether solid or open-sided, before assembling the sides cut a horizontal piece from the apex end of each triangle that is the length of the crystal pyramid base. When building an open-frame pyramid, be sure the plywood triangles at the apex are larger than the crystal pyramid – otherwise there will be no way to connect the sides.

After acquiring a pyramid in whatever size or material, the next consideration is how to use it. Stone or glass 'crystal' pyramids can be used in a number of ways. The most obvious use is to simply hold it in the hands. A mild word of caution though: the writer has on two separate occasions seen demonstrations of the reality of 'pyramid power' with small natural stone pyramids! In one instance a small pyramid was dropped into a person's hand, and the person immediately flung it straight into the air with a scream. She said it was like having a red-hot coal dropped into her hand. This was a person not connected in any way with esoterics or the occult, and the result could not have been more unexpected. She reluctantly agreed to try again with a pyramid of another material – with exactly the same result.

In another instance, a member of the public at an exhibition and totally unknown to the writer, was handed a small pyramid of the green stone chrysoprase; their right arm immediately went numb to the elbow. After a few uncomfortable moments for both of us, the numbness began to fade, although it was nearly a half hour before it was gone entirely. The explanation? Pyramid power? Past lives? In truth, it is impossible to say exactly. These were but two of perhaps a thousand people who have handled such pyramids in the presence of the author; but there is no doubt about the authenticity of the reactions. The caution? Approach the use of such objects gently, and be aware that there may be reactions. They are almost certainly not going to be harmful.

A number of communities and centres which have meditation rooms have placed crystal pyramids at the top-centre of the room, so that anyone meditating there is underneath whatever influence the pyramid may have. Individuals have created meditation pyramids for themselves, rather like the commercially available ones, as described here. At the top of these open-framed pyramids provision is made to place a crystal pyramid, so the meditation takes place

directly beneath it. Small pyramids can be suspended over the bed while sleeping, placed beneath the bed, or even under the pillow if the pyramid is small enough. An open-frame pyramid can be constructed that is large enough to fit over the upper end of a bed. One of the base pieces is left out and that side of the pyramid is braced from higher up in its structure, which allows the sleeping person to lie inside it without the base piece across their back. However you use your pyramid, the best results can be expected if one face of your pyramid is oriented to the north. A cheap compass is good enough to get a close orientation.

On a yet larger scale, you may actually wish to visit some of the ancient pyramids described in this book. A few of them are quite easy to get to, others require varying degrees of effort. In Egypt, the Giza pyramids are very easy to reach. There are frequent flights to Cairo, where you can jump in a taxi, and within an hour be inside the Great Pyramid. There is a hotel at the base of the Giza plateau, and other hotels in Cairo can arrange visits. The Egyptian Tourist Board can be contacted directly or your local travel agent can find information for you. This is also true of the pyramids in Mexico, the largest of which are easily accessible from Mexico City. The Pyramids of the Sun and Moon at Teotihuacan are roughly 48 kilometres from Mexico City, and again large city hotels can arrange tours. The Mexican Tourist Board is very helpful and can also provide information about travel to the Maya areas of southern Mexico and Yucatan. There are scheduled flights to both Merida and Cozumel, from where access to a number of Maya pyramids, including the Pyramid of Kukulcan at Chichen Itza, is possible. Palenque, a bit further south and west of Chichen Itza and Tikal in Guatemala, are somewhat less accessible, but again the tourist boards are helpful with up-to-date information.

When arranging visits to any of these places, be aware that in some instances there are local political problems which may pose some degree of hazard to the traveller. Always check about the local situation before finalizing any plans.

A Pyramid visualization

The pyramid is a singularly powerful image. Pyramids combine the symbolism of the Mother Mountain with the primordial womb in their inner chambers. Thus, as an archetypal symbol for use in visualization, they are unsurpassed for tapping into ancient wisdom – wisdom that is part of our forgotten, but inbuilt, human heritage.

Some readers may have no experience either of visualization or meditation. For those readers, a brief word: meditation and visualization are simply forms of relaxation. Remember, you are in complete control of your experience, and can stop at any time. It is not hypnosis or anything similar: it is just relaxation. During your time of relaxation, you simply suggest an image to yourself, a symbol, and follow it through to its conclusion. The human mind works very much in symbols, and by creating appropriate symbols our subconscious mind will grasp them quickly, and begin making the perceptual shifts necessary for further personal growth.

There are several steps in a visualization. Creating a personal, sacred space is a good beginning, whether you meditate in it or simply experience and bring forth what you are and what you might be. It can be a room, a certain hour in the day, or music that you love. It is often called a place of creative incubation.

When you are in your space, make yourself comfortable. Sit on a chair or on the floor, and arrange your legs in the most comfortable position. Take a deep breath and let it out slowly. Do the same again. Relax, and focus on the rise and fall of your chest. Your eyes will close of their own accord, and your breathing will start to slow. You are practising a relaxation technique that is good for dealing with stress, and you can use it for that at any time, even in the office. When you are ready, you can start your visualization.

A general format is suggested here, but you can vary it to suit. In the sacred space inside the pyramid you can seek answers to any of your life's problems or questions. You can invite in people with whom you have unresolved issues, or people you have missed a chance to speak to at an appropriate time, like a deceased friend; or perhaps

someone from a past relationship where important words were left unsaid. In the inner sanctuary of a pyramid, the limitations of time and space are diminished, and you can do much inner work. Alternatively, just use it for relaxation and renewal.

pRACTICE

1 To start, close your eyes and find yourself standing at the head of an avenue lined on both sides with sphinxes, and leading to the entrance of a pyramid.

2 When the moment comes to start your journey, walk towards the pyramid, being aware of the soft, warm breeze and, with the exception of the sound of your footsteps on the stone pathway, the utter stillness.

3 As you reach the corridor into the centre of the pyramid, it is lit with torches, and as you enter, the cool stone surrounds you. As you walk further inward, you reach the doorway to the inner chamber, and enter.

4 The chamber is lit by a single candle. In the exact centre of the chamber is a single chair, where you sit.

5 As you sit quietly, begin to sense the expanse of the pyramid around you, and then the world beyond it. It will take on an actual physical sensation, as if you yourself have expanded, and are more connected to all that surrounds you. It is through this connection to the surrounding world that life is able to know and respond to our deepest needs. Remember that life responds to our real needs, and not necessarily to our wishes and desires. This is the moment to make your need known, either out loud or silently, but speaking to the whole of life that surrounds you. Take all the time you need in this step.

6 Know that the path to the truth is an unfolding process, and life will only provide you with whatever serves you best at the time. It even may appear that nothing has happened, but don't worry – life never refuses a request for truth.

7 When you feel a sense of completion with the process, take a few deep breaths, and become aware of your surroundings again. When you are ready, your eyes will open naturally.

Conclusion

We have explored many of the ideas, beliefs, and theories surrounding the pyramids and their mysteries. As we can see, there is still much to learn. And are there more pyramids yet to find? Without a doubt: unknown pyramids are still coming to light. In 1996 Jaime Cortes-Hernandez, state archaeologist for Veracruz, Mexico, uncovered a major ceremonial site at Caujilote. Within the site is a whole avenue of pyramids, built between AD 400 and 800 (*National Geographic*, 2 August 1996). Given that virtually all of the Maya region is covered with thick jungle, as is much of the 'pyramid country' both further north in central Mexico and further south in Guatemala and Honduras, there may be literally dozens yet to be found.

Even in Egypt pyramids are still being discovered. It wasn't until 1950 that the ruined and unfinished Pyramid of Sekhemket was finally revealed at Dashur, in the middle of a major pyramid field! Other pyramids are known from inscriptions, but have not yet been found: the Pyramid of Shepseskare is probably either at or near Saqqara or Abusir, but no trace of it has yet emerged. Likewise the Pyramid of Menkauhor lies somewhere in the same area, but again, it has not been located. Aerial photographs along the major pyramid fields of the Nile show buried shapes that may well be yet other undiscovered pyramids.

Is the Age of Pyramids over? Judge for yourself: the last pyramid to be built is actually the fourth largest in the world. When was it built? In the 1980s. Where is it? In Las Vegas, Nevada. It is a hotel and casino.

REFERENCES AND FURTHER READING

REFERENCES

Bauval, Robert and Gilbert, Adrian *The Orion Mystery* (London: Heinemann, 1994).

Bonewitz, Ronald *The Timeless Wisdom of the Egyptians* (London: Hodder & Stoughton, 1999).

Cummings, Byron S. 'Cuicilco and Archaic Culture of Mexico' (University of Arizona, Volume IV: 8, 15 November 1933).

Donelly, Ignatius *North America of Antiquity*, p.286. Cited in: *Atlantis: The Antediluvian World* (New York: Harper Bros., 1882).

Duran, Diego 'Historia Antiqua de la Nueve España' (1585), in Ignatius Donelly, *Atlantis: the Antediluvian World* (New York: Harper and Brothers, 1882).

Gauquelin, Michel *The Cosmic Clocks* (London: Peter Owen, 1967).

Hancock, Graham *Fingerprints of the Gods* (London: Mandarin, 1995).

Irwin, *Constance Fair Gods and Stone Faces*, (London: W.H. Allen, 1964).

Lichthetim, Miriam *Ancient Egyptian Literature*, Volume II (University of California Press, 1976).

Morley, Sylvanus Griswold *An Introduction to the Study of Maya Hieroglyphics* (New York: Dover Publications, 1975).

Murray, H., Crawford J. et al *An Historical and Descriptive Account of China* (second edition, 1836, Volume 1).

Neugebaure, O. and Parker, R. *Egyptian Astronomical Texts*, (Volume 1, Brown University Press, London: Lund Humphries, 1964).

Speake, Graham Ed. *Atlas of Ancient Egypt* (Oxford: Equinox, 1980).

Stuart, George E. 'Etowah', *National Geographic* (Volume 180, No. 4, October 1991).

Sullivan, William *The Secret of the Incas* (New York: Crown, 1996).

Tedlock, Dennis, trans. *The Popol Vuh* (London: Simon and Schuster, 1996).

Tompkins, Peter *Secrets of the Great Pyramid* (London: Penguin, 1978).

Tompkins, Peter *Mysteries of the Mexican Pyramids* (London: Thames and Hudson, 1987).

'Secrets of the Cloud People', *QED*, Prod. Jan Klimkowski, BBC, 1998.

'Uncovering a Ritual Center in Veracruz', *National Geographic* (Volume 190, No. 2, August 1996).

fURThER READING

Bauval, Robert and Gilbert, Adrian *The Orion Mystery* (London: Heinemann, 1994).

Bonewitz, Ronald *The Timeless Wisdom of the Egyptians* (London: Hodder & Stoughton, 1999).

Coe, Michael, *The Maya* (London: Thames and Hudson,1993).

Hancock, Graham *Fingerprints of the Gods* (London: Mandarin, 1995).

Henderson, John, *The World of the Ancient Maya* (London: John Murray, 1997).

Miller, Mary, and Taube, Karl *The Gods and Symbols of Ancient Mexico* (London: Thames and Hudson, 1993).

Tedlock, Dennis, trans. *The Popol Vuh* (London: Simon and Schuster, 1996).